PHL

54060000301753

THE
**PAUL HAMLYN
LIBRARY**

————•————

DONATED BY

THE PAUL HAMLYN

FOUNDATION

TO THE

BRITISH MUSEUM

————•————

Opened December 2000

D1580362

THE THEORY OF ETERNAL LIFE

THE THEORY OF
ETERNAL LIFE

by Rodney Collin

LONDON

VINCENT STUART

FIRST LIMITED EDITION
BY THE STOURTON PRESS, CAPE TOWN, 1950
FIRST PUBLISHED IN THIS EDITION
BY VINCENT STUART PUBLISHERS LTD
55 WELBECK STREET LONDON WI.
ALL RIGHTS RESERVED
1956

MADE AND PRINTED
IN GREAT BRITAIN
BY ROBERT CUNNINGHAM AND SONS LTD
ALVA
CLACKMANNANSHIRE

THE BRITISH MUSEUM
THE PAUL HAMLYN LIBRARY

129 COL

CONTENTS

Life is a lyre, for its tune is death. LXVI

Immortal mortals and mortal immortals—one living LXVII
the other's death and dead the other's life. For it is
death to the breath of life to become liquid, and death LXVIII
to this liquid to become solid. But from such solid
comes liquid and from such liquid the breath of life.

The path up and the path down is one and the same. LXI
Identical the beginning and the end... Living and dead LXX
are the same, and so awake and asleep, young and old: LXXVIII
the former shifted become the latter, and the latter
shifted the former.

For time is a child playing draughts, and that child's LXXIX
is the move.

HERACLEITUS: On the Universe

To him who, purified, would break this vicious round
And breathe once more the air of heaven—greeting!
There in the courts of hades wilt thou find
Leftward a beckoning cypress, tall and bright,
From out whose root doth flow the water of Oblivion.
Approach it not: guard thou thy thirst awhile.
For on the other hand—and further—wells
From bottomless pool the limpid stream of Memory,
Cool, full of refreshment. To its guardians cry thus:
'I am the child of earth and starry sky:
Know that I too am heavenly—but parched!
I perish: give then and quickly that clear draught
Of ice-cold Memory!' And from that fountainhead divine
Straightway they'll give thee drink; quaffing the which
Thou with the other heroes eternally shalt rule.

Golden Tablet found in an Orphic Tomb

vi

The Bargain between Nachiketas and Death

Nachiketas said: 'Some say that when man dies he continues to exist, others that he does not. Explain, and that shall be my third gift.'

Death said: 'This question has been discussed by the gods, it is deep and difficult. Choose another gift, Nachiketas! Do not be hard. Do not compel me to explain.'

Nachiketas said: 'Death! you say that the gods have discussed it, that it is deep and difficult; what explanation can be as good as yours? What gift compares with that?'

Death said: 'Take sons and grandsons, all long-lived, cattle and horses, elephants and gold, take a great kingdom.

'Anything but this; wealth, long life, Nachiketas! empire, anything whatever; satisfy the heart's desire.

'Pleasures beyond human reach, fine women with carriages, their musical instruments; mount beyond dreams; enjoy. But do not ask what lies beyond death.'

Nachiketas said: 'Destroyer of man! these things pass. Joy ends enjoyment, the longest life is short. Keep those horses, keep singing and dancing, keep it all for yourself.

'Wealth cannot satisfy a man. If he but please you, Master of All, he can live as long as he likes, get all that he likes; but I will not change my gift.

'What man, subject to death and decay, getting the chance of undecaying life, would still enjoy mere long life, thinking of copulation and beauty?

'Say where man goes after death; end all that discussion. This, which you have made so mysterious, is the only gift I will take.'

*Katha-Upanishad**

* From *Ten Principal Upanishads* by Shree Purohit Swāmi and W. B. Yeats. By kind permission of Mrs Yeats, Messrs Faber and Faber Ltd. and the Macmillan Company

I

LIFE BETWEEN BIRTH AND DEATH*

MAN is born and man dies. Between these two points lies a line of development which is called life.

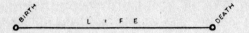

But birth is not the beginning for a man. For at this point the physical vehicle which determines what he will be is already formed. Its strong and weak points, its innate inclinations and potentialities, are already established. In reality, man's individual career has begun much earlier, at conception—thus:

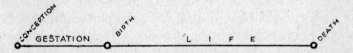

How should this line of man's career be measured? Counted in years, gestation is but a hundredth part of it. But measurement in years is a planetary scale, created by the motion of the earth, and does not refer to the inner time of man. To measure his organic development we must find quite a different scale. The clue to this new scale lies in the fact that man is conceived as a single cell, under the laws and time-scale of the world of cells: but he ends as a human being, with eighty years of memory behind him, under the laws and time-scale of men.

This means that during the course of his career he passes all the way from cellular time to human time. He lives on a

* This chapter represents an extreme condensation of the ideas contained in Chapters 10, 11, 14 and 21 of an earlier book, *The Theory of Celestial Influence*

sliding or logarithmic scale of time. His inner processes, launched with almost unimaginable speed at the moment of conception, run slower and slower, like a clockwork mechanism running down, until their complete cessation in death. On this scale of work done, the period of gestation constitutes not a hundredth, but a third of man's career.

From another point of view, this period may be taken as the time of formation of one-third of man's total nature. This third, the grossest part of his final psycho-physical organism, consists of its original physical vehicle or *organic body*. After birth a man's body may be kept healthy or made ill, one or another function may be developed or left dormant. But it can never be made into a different body from that already created. A round-headed infant can never grow into a long-headed man, nor a brown-eyed one into a blue-eyed adult. Both the fundamental physical make-up and the reactions which spring from it are already fully determined at birth.

The formation of the second part of man's nature, his *personality*, takes place during a second period called childhood. During this time the physical body made before birth establishes relations with the outside world. It comes to regard certain surroundings as natural, familiar and reassuring; others as strange and forbidding. These constitute its normality. While within this given framework its own innate physical tendencies establish an individual taste in companions, pastimes, seasons, places, and so on. Towards the end of childhood comes the ability to think in concepts, and its civilized corollary, the art of reading. And among the infinite number of worlds of the imagination so made available, the individual will choose or have chosen for him one or two which will ever after influence the scenery of his mind.

By the end of childhood, the personality—which is as it were the intermediary between the naked physical organism and the world in which it exists—is already formed. This surrounding world is infinite, but the personality so grown in childhood, like a tinted filter, ensures that the grown man shall see it always tinted a certain colour, with all objects of that colour greatly heightened in value and objects of other colours diminished or eliminated altogether. This personality forms a definite and enduring part of man's organism, and after adolescence is not seriously affected until death. This principle is recognized by many religious and political ideologies which insist on close control over young children up to the age of seven or ten, when their 'indoctrination' is regarded as secure.

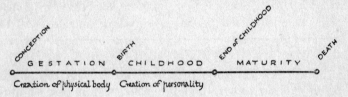

During the remainder of life, from about seven years to the end of man's term, the dual organism of body and personality works out all its possible reactions to the circumstances in which it may find itself. This period, called maturity, is in most cases an automatic result of the exposure of the being already created to new problems, places and people, and does not involve the creation of anything new in itself.

The meaning of these three periods of existence for man may be explained by the analogy of a statue. In the first period the statue is carved from stone or wood: in the second it is painted, decorated and inset with jewels: in the third period the finished image passes from hand to hand, is cherished by an appreciative owner, lies neglected on a rubbish-heap, is now clean, now dirty, now despoiled of its jewels, now even redecorated. Yet until the moment of its final destruction by wantonness, accident or decay, it remains the same statue as was delivered into the world from the craftsman's workshop.

Thus with ordinary man. But we have evidence to suggest that this third period is *potentially* that of the development of a third and normally latent part of man's nature. We may call this the *soul*. Later we shall see why it may be said that ordinary man has only a dormant soul, and why the awakening of the soul may be regarded as the most difficult task a man can possibly set himself—comparable, in fact, to the transformation of the statue into a living being.

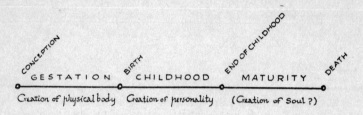

How can we understand the scale of this line of life in which gestation, childhood and maturity are of equal content? What does this slowing down of vital processes signify? What is the relation between the organic time shown upon this scale, and the time of months and years in which human age is usually measured?

Imagine a top which with a normal impulse spins for 75 seconds. At the moment of launching, this top spins at the rate of many dozen revolutions a second: in the last second before it falls motionless it may complete only a single turn. The scale of seconds represents our ordinary measurement of man's time by years: the scale of revolutions represents work done, for it is each revolution not each second which represents a fixed amount of energy spent. In this way scores of times more work is done in the first second than the last. And so with the years of man's life.

Let us place an average duration upon the three periods of life already described. Human gestation lasts 280 days or 10 lunar months; childhood about seven years or 100 lunar months; while man's traditional span of life, between 70 and 80 years, is equivalent to 1000 lunar months.

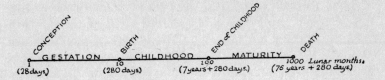

Such a scale, covering in equal distances 1, 10, 100 and 1000 units, is called a logarithmic scale. Using such a scale consistently, we can obtain finer divisions on a basis of equal organic work:

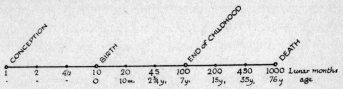

In this way man's existence is divided into nine parts, each of which lasts slightly longer than all the time that went before.

Further, each part marks the ascendancy of one function of his organism. All such functions are present in man, either potentially or operatively, throughout his whole life. But at each milestone one dominates his organism, controls it, and lends the corresponding age its own particular colour.

At two months from conception the embryo is nothing but a digesting organism, a machine for transmuting the nourishment received in the bloodstream of the mother into the cellular tissue of a certain form. Of all the functions later familiar to the adult man—digestion, motion, respiration, instinctive metabolism, thought, passionate emotion, and creative function or sex—only the first is fully realized in the embryo at this stage. Point 1 on this logarithmic scale may thus be said to be dominated by the function of *digestion*.

At four and a half months from conception a new function begins to develop. This is connected with respiration and movement, which are in fact two aspects of the same thing—respiration determining tempo of movement and vice versa, as in the relation between the draught of a locomotive furnace and the potential speed of the train. At this moment the embryo acquires individual movement or quickens, as we say, and thereafter its lung-system begins to develop in readiness for the commencement of breathing at the instant of birth. Thus at point 2 we may say that the function of *motion* enters and at point 3 that of *respiration*.

In the first year of life the physical metabolism connected with the growth of tissue and increase in volume is at its most vigorous. In this year the infant gains more weight than in any other single year of its existence. All the best energies of the organism now appear to go into the *metabolism of physical growth*, which, for want of a better description, we may call the function characteristic of point 4.

At point 5, between two-and-a-half and three years, rapid growth of the brain gives ascendancy to the *intellectual function;* the child acquires the power of speech and of abstract concepts; and through the intellectual grouping of impressions, culminating in the capacity to reason, gradually forms personality. In a general way point 6 marks the completion of this process.

Point 7 or fifteen years marks puberty, in which the combination of adrenal and sex glands come into play, and between them excite the organism to *passionate emotion* and its projection. Such projection should be distinguished from true sex which is consciously creative in its nature; while this is more connected with the violent, aggressive and passionate urges which peculiarly mark adolescence, but for many people remain their highest expression even in maturity.

True sex, in the sense of the highest *creative function*, which results in the harmonizing of all other functions—whether in creation of children in the physical image of their parents, in the creation of the arts, or in the creation of the individual's true role in life—is fulfilled only with the development of higher emotions at point 8, the prime of life. But the full expression of this function is dependent on the growth of new powers and new capacities, potential in man but only realizable with very special work and knowledge. The key to these new powers lies in the possibility of man becoming conscious of himself and of his place in the surrounding universe. For from this may arise—in very fortunate cases— a fully-formed *soul*, or permanent principle of consciousness.

In the ordinary way, there is neither permanence nor consciousness in man. Each of these functions speaks in him, automatically and in turn, with a different voice, for its own interests, indifferent to the interests of the others, its the whole, yet using the tongue and the name of the or of individual.

'I must read the paper!' intellectual function says. 'I'll go riding!' motor function contradicts. 'I'm hungry!' declares digestion; 'I'm cold!' metabolism. And 'I'll not be thwarted!' cries passionate emotion, in the defence of any of them.

Such are the many 'I's of man. And in them lies the key to all the inner and outer contradiction, which plunges him into such confusion, cancels his best intentions, and keeps him busy paying the debts recklessly incurred by each of his many sides. Each function of his essence, as well as each imagination of his personality, makes promises, incurs obligations, for which the man as a whole must accept responsibility.

Thus the first condition for a soul, or unifying principle, lies in the gradual confinement of each function to its proper rôle, through self-observation and awareness, and the gradual removal of contradictions between them through their common recognition of this single aim.

A summary of the functions which enter at successive points on the line of man's life, will thus show that though from one point of view his life is running down as he grows older, from another point of view new powers working with finer energies and having ever greater possibilities periodically unfold in him.

Point	Age	New Function	System
1	2 months from conception	Digestive	Alimentary
2	4½ months from conception	Motor	Muscular
3	Birth	Respiratory (Completion of physical body)	Pulmonary
4	10½ months	Metabolism of growth	Connective tissue
5	2¾ years	Intellectual	Cerebro-spinal
6	7 years	(Completion of personality)	
7	15 years	Passionate emotion	Sympathetic nervous
8	35 years	Sex: creative emotion	Reproductive and vagus

These functions represent the action in man of different levels of energy, each of which has its own appropriate system in the human body. In exactly the same way the different energies or matters which circulate in a house—hot and cold water, gas, electric light and electric power—are each carried by their own system of pipes or wires. But although these systems exist in the organism of man from his very earliest days, the energy or matter which operates through them is only released by nature at a certain age, just as the water, gas and electricity serving the house might be turned on from their appropriate mains on different and successive dates.

Now the characteristic of all the above-mentioned functions and their energies is that they work in an organic body, through organs and tissues of cellular structure. This is self-evident. For even though the higher emotions produce phenomena which appear to be super-physical, we yet know that they are conveyed by a tangible brain and nervous system whose structure we can examine. Nor can we normally conceive their operation apart from this physical machine.

Yet we have every reason to believe that the impact of ever higher energies at successive stages of development does not end at point 8, or the prime of life. At point 9 of a logarithmic scale, which is equivalent to about seventy-five or seventy-six years, a still higher and more penetrating energy is projected into man's existence by nature.

But this energy differs from the others in that it is *too intense* to be contained within a body of cellular structure; in just the same way that the energy of lightning is too intense to be contained within the body of a tree, which when struck is immediately blasted and destroyed. This final cosmic energy is of such a nature that at its impact the cellular body of man is immediately split off from any more enduring life-principle which may exist in him, and is left to disintegrate. This phenomenon appears to him as death.

Negatively, this supreme energy destroys the physical or organic body of man. But what does it positively do? We may say that *it connects death and conception*. This means that it is of such a nature that *it works outside our time*. Through it the final sum or essential signature of an individual is conveyed *back* to the moment when the chromosomes of the fertilized ovum perform the pairing-dance by which all the subsequent qualities of his organism are to be determined.

How can this be? Our sense of *time* derives from the physiological unfolding of the body, just as our sense of *warmth* derives from the temperature of the blood. The cellular body is both our clock and our thermometer. The shock which destroys it frees us simultaneously from temperature and from time.

At death we enter timelessness or eternity. From that state of timelessness, from that enjoyment of eternity, all points within time are equally accessible. Or rather they are

B

related, not by time, but by *the intensity of the energy which informs them*.

Two points in the normal cycle of human life are informed by the most potent and divine energy we know. Only God gives life and only God takes it. Death and conception are connected outside time by the divine intensity of the energy involved. Just as one magnet, another magnet and the North Pole are connected outside time by their common magnetism: so death, conception and God are connected outside time by their common potency.

The energy of death reduces man's total being, the product of all his days, to an invisible quintessence, as distillation may reduce tens of thousands of flowers to a single drop of essential perfume. And just as this perfume has the power of passing through the crack of a door, in a way which would be inconceivable for the flowers in their original physical form, so the essence of man distilled by death appears able to pass through time in a way quite inconceivable from the point of view of his organic body.

So is the death-agony of a man identical with the ecstasy of his conception; and what he has become at the former moment must control that which will inevitably spring from the pattern created at the latter.

Our figure now assumes the form shown opposite.

What may be said of man's ordinary perception of his life in such a scheme? What is the nature of his consciousness and of his memory of what has happened to him? Man's ordinary awareness of his existence may be seen as a feeble point of light or warmth which travels inexorably round this circle from birth to death, barely sufficient to cast its radiance more than a day or two before and behind, yet sometimes leaving in its wake a certain residual energy which we feel as memory.

To this progress of consciousness and memory in the feeble state in which they exist in ordinary man, however, the point at the summit of the circle represents an insuperable barrier. Past this insulator of death and conception the

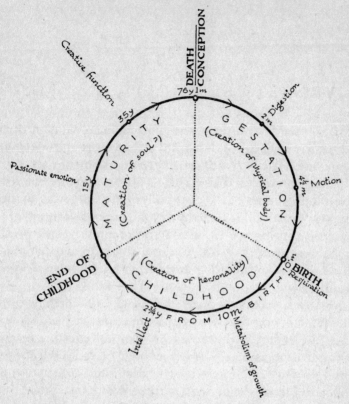

consciousness of ordinary man may not pass; and of what lies beyond that, either ahead or behind, his memory tells him nothing.

Yet because this is the greatest of all mysteries, we may not ignore it. All must come sooner or later to that point, and it were better that they come there with all the faculty of understanding available to them in life focussed thereon, rather than blindly and in fear. For from fear nothing but ill may be expected to befall.

II

LIVES BETWEEN DEATH AND BIRTH

IT is possible to come to the conclusion, as we have done, that the moment of death and the moment of conception are one. The very tearing apart of the constituents of the old body produces that electric tension which causes the determining genes of the next body to rush together in their new combination. It is as though the note or *chord* set up by the man's being in its mortal disintegration causes the subtle constituents of the fertilized ovum to arrange themselves in a corresponding pattern, as the note of a violin produces a corresponding pattern on a sand-tray.

And this occurs because the energy of death and the energy of conception are of the same intensity and subtleness—an energy so penetrating that its effects can pass through time as easily as the energy of radio-waves pass through space. The reason why death and conception are united in this way is because at these two points and at these only there enters into the existence of ordinary man this god-like time-penetrating energy. All the energies that automatically work in man between conception and death, even the most intense, are of such a nature that their effect is confined to one point of time; just as the effect of mechanical energy, a lever, for example, is confined to one point of space. The higher energy of death and conception, on the other hand, instantaneously diffuses through long tracts of time; just as electro-magnetic energy, such as light or radio-waves, instantaneously diffuses through vast areas of space. But the signature or record of life released at death, even though it be free of time, finds no other place in man's existence sufficiently sensitive to receive its imprint, but conception. It is in this sense that death and conception may be regarded as one and simultaneous.

Now this moment of death and conception is inevitably connected with the idea of the Judgment. We are familiar with the opening of the tombs, the last trump, the weighing of souls, the division into damned and blessed of the mediaeval picture. But all true teachings include this idea, very often in much more subtle and detailed form. In a book called *The Night Side of Nature*, it is said: 'The instant the soul is forced from the body it sees its whole earthly career in a single sign; it knows that it is good or evil, and pronounces its own sentence.' Here the idea of self-judgment is made very clear. Put in a mechanistic way this means that judgment or determination of future state is *an exact mathematical resultant* of the causes set up in the past life. This is conveyed even more graphically by certain Sankhya descriptions.

In Plato's strange myth of Er the Pamphylian, who was taken up for dead in battle, and twelve days later, when already lying on the funeral pyre, came to life again, it is described how the souls of men go on a long journey, encamping at last in a meadow between the mouths of heaven and hell. Here, after witnessing the going up and casting down of souls according to their deserts, they are vouchsafed a vision of the Three Fates—those of the past, present and future. From the lap of Lachesis, Fate of the Past, are thrown down innumerable examples of lives, which the souls choose according to their nature and desire —but most after the custom of their former life.

Here is introduced the idea that *something could be altered at the Judgment*. If a man could arrive there with full knowledge of what he has been and what he wants to be, choice would be open to him. Only most men cannot conceive a different life, they are bound to choose what is familiar; so that for them there is in fact no choice.

In the Christian vision of St. Makary of Alexandria (third century), the soul was seen for three days being helped free from the body by its guardian angel. It then ascended to God for adoration, was sent for six days to experience the delights of paradise, ascended a second time to God, was condemned to wander thirty days in hell, and only on the fortieth day came to final judgment.

Again in the *Tibetan Book of the Dead*, the bodiless self is said to pass three and a half days in swoon, to be raised to ultimate bliss or buddhahood for an hour, after which it comes gradually descending through the invisible worlds until—some time after the eighteenth day—it reaches judgment and the very entrance of that womb from which it will next be born. All the hierarchy of Gods attend this Judgment, at which the mirror of karma or the soul's own past is the final witness.

Now the *Tibetan Book of the Dead* makes clear openly what all the other versions innerly suggest—namely, that Judgment is the assignment to the disembodied self of a new body in accordance with its record. Until this Judgment the soul can always hope through some final act of adoration or understanding to improve its future lot. But Judgment once made can never be reversed, and the self now endowed with its new vehicle must pass through the whole cycle of that body's life, before it comes again to the same court and the same chance.

What else can this mean but conception? Nothing can turn back the unfolding of a body once conceived, nor change the nature and capacities inherent in it. Such capacities may be used well or ill, they may be cultivated or atrophy, but they cannot be exchanged for others, nor can one be rid of them.

Death and conception are one. Death and Judgment are one. Judgment and conception are one. Death, Judgment and conception are one. This is the closing of the circle of life.

There is, however, an idea that we have completely omitted from our reading of these strange texts. According to St. Makary the soul passes forty days in heaven, hell and paradise between death and judgment. The soul of Er the Pamphylian remembered camping for seven days in the celestial meadow, then journeying for four days more before it came to the vision of the Fates and the distribution of lives. In the *Tibetan Book of the Dead* from eighteen to forty days, each with its own appropriate visions and experience, elapse between Judgment and re-entry into the womb.

All these accounts agree in suggesting that there is *a definite interval*, exactly measurable by days or weeks, between Death and Judgment. During this time the self is bodiless, and in this state is able to perceive *as real* different parts of the cosmos unattainable to it when attached to a body. But how can death, judgment and conception be simultaneous, and yet separated by an immensely important interval? This is the greatest mystery.

An interesting point now comes to mind from our diagram. Since it was a logarithmic scale which we found to fit best with the pattern of life, and since the three equal divisions of physical existence are in this way marked by 1, 10, 100 and 1000 months, the beginning of the circle or conception occurs not at zero but at 1. Somewhere, *not included in the circle*, is a missing month. But this circle, by our definition, represents the life of the body. The missing month is therefore passed outside the circle of the body. And, moreover, on our logarithmic scale, *this month is as long as all the rest of existence*. It is the invisible and infinite interval between two iden-

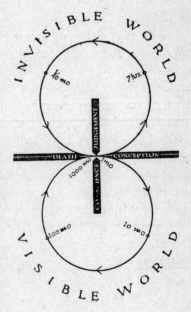

tical points. Death and conception are one; yet between them lies a whole existence. This is only possible in another dimension.

How can this be represented? There is one way: This is the figure of infinity—two connecting circles, one belonging to the physical world and one to the next, one invisible and one visible. Seen from the physical world, the visible circle looks complete in itself. It is perfect and without entrance or exit. It is the *vicious circle of man's life*. At the same time its only meaning comes from its contact with the invisible circle into which the soul passes at the moment of death, and in which it lives a full, complete existence before being conceived into a new body, at the self-same moment.

This too is the secret of Plato's myth in the *Politicus*, in which it is explained how for a certain time the cosmos is propelled by God in a circular motion, and then, the cycle of time appointed to it being accomplished, it is released and begins to go round in the contrary direction, but this time of itself as an independent living creature.* There could be no better description of the relation between the invisible and visible circles.

About the pattern of this invisible existence we can even make deductions. We already realized that life moves slower and slower as it passes from conception to death. Human existence thus represents no one time, but a long slowing down of time from the speed of cellular life which controls conception to the speed of mental life which dominates at death. Looking back towards conception we see everything happening faster and faster, more and more experience filling each unit of time. At the end of childhood experience is tenfold more compressed than in old age, at birth a hundredfold, and at conception a thousandfold.

At conception the speed of experience has reached the ultimate limit for cellular life—that is, the fastest possible within the confines of a physical body. If the progression be continued further it will be *too fast to be contained within a*

* The Myths of Plato, trs. by J. A. Stewart, p. 179

cellular form; it becomes akin to the speed of molecular energy. This is the nature of experience in the invisible circle.

We can by deduction continue our scale backwards into this second circle, even though we cannot see or measure it. If by analogy we divide this circle again into three periods, these periods will be marked by one month, one-tenth of a month (2·8 days), one-hundredth of a month (7 hours), and one-thousandth of a month (40 minutes). And again, *these periods will be equal in content*.

But still we are left with forty minutes missing. And just as in considering the circle of the life of the physical body we could find no place for the missing month, save outside the physical world, so here also we have to suppose a world in yet another dimension. The whole circle of this dimension will last but forty minutes—the 'mealtime period' immediately following expiration, during which, according to the *Tibetan Book of the Dead*, the 'primary Clear Light' of perfect Buddhahood dawns on the escaping soul. This circle is the world of the higher mental centre as the last was the world of the higher emotional centre. It is the electronic world of

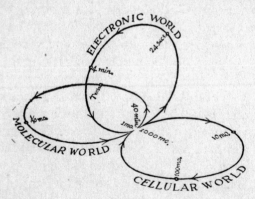

light, as that was the molecular world of essence. This circle lies in the third dimension of time, where all possibilities are realized.

Even within this circle we can conceive the same extraordinary scale continuing. So that the three divisions of this third circle will be marked by 40 minutes, 4 minutes, 24 seconds and 2½ seconds. All these periods will again be equal to each other, and to all those that went before. And it is in the final point of this circle, or a single breath, the uttermost limit of compression of experience where all is *a billion times* faster and finer than in the world of the physical body, that the dying man may see his whole life 'as a single sign'.

From this we can understand one aspect of higher worlds —they are worlds in which the same amount is known or experienced in shorter time. The characteristic of the ordinary logical mind by whose speed is measured the life of the physical body is that *one thing is known or experienced after another*. When logical mind passes on to the next experience it is unable to retain the experience or knowledge which went before. This it must leave behind. For the logical mind all proofs are made sequentially or *in time*. But by the time it reaches the end of its proof logical mind has already lost sight of the beginning, *because things can only pass through it in succession*. From this arise all the phenomena of forgetfulness. Relying on the logical mind alone, *man must forget*.

It is not that man's life does not contain enough experience or knowledge for him to become wise or illuminated. But relying on the perception of logical mind, he only experiences one thing at a time, and forgets this as soon as he passes on to the next. If all that he knows at one time or another could be compressed into shorter time, so that less was forgotten, innumerable connections of cause and effect, and patterns of cosmic influence would appear, which would render him wise beyond imagination.

This is what appears to happen in the higher and invisible worlds into which the self penetrates at death. In the second circle the equivalent of a whole lifetime of experience passes in one month: in the third circle the same is compressed into forty minutes: and in the ultimate point of this circle a lifetime is lived in two and a half seconds.

Let us try to imagine what such compression could mean. In the *Tibetan Book of the Dead*, which is supposedly addressed to the soul of the dead man, to guide him in his wanderings through the invisible world, it is again and again emphasized that everything he may meet—ecstasies, terrors, dazzling light, black darkness, gods and demons—all comes from *his own mind*. It is himself that he encounters, all that he is. If he can understand this he can become free.

From this, it is further emphasized that for men of each race the invisible worlds will appear and be peopled according to the tenets of their earthly belief; and that even for men of no belief these worlds will be in some way a tremendously intensified vision of that which occupied their minds in life. Individual karma is intensely compressed and then seen through the lens of beliefs, so that all that is within him of good and evil appears to one man as an assembly of angels and devils, to another as mathematical laws made visible, to a third as beneficent and terrible forces of nature, to a fourth as living symbols, to a fifth as a nightmare of unnamed fears and phantoms, and so on.

This idea, which is found in many interpretations of heaven and hell, seems to suggest that the ecstatic or appalling appearance of the invisible worlds could be explained simply by *an intense compression of a soul's own life experience*.

Some idea of the meaning of such compression can be gained even from a study of the subjective effect of ordinary emotions. For whereas the logical mind perceives ideas and experiences only in succession, the emotions make possible the reception of ideas and experiences *simultaneously*. One suddenly sees a near friend or a child weeping: *instantly and simultaneously* there pass through one's emotional perception a hundred memories of cruelties inflicted, irreparable losses, bitter insults, all combined with the sensation of *one's own fault* or of *someone else's fault*, and again with images of compassion and tenderness drawn from scripture, art, the lives of saints or even from parents or others in one's own circle. If the emotional reaction is sufficiently strong all these memories may instantaneously combine to produce an almost overwhelming sensation of pity, indignation, poignancy and fear.

Now if some dozens or hundreds of images perceived together by ordinary emotion yield such effect, what would be the effect of a *lifetime of billions of images* compressed into an hour, a minute or a second? We can only say that if the life had been filled with pleasant emotions, pleasant encounters, pleasant impressions of people and nature, apprehensions of truth, discoveries of natural law, creative work, affection, courage, honesty and so on, the effect of such compression would be ecstatic beyond imagination. If, on the other hand, the life had been filled with the infliction of cruelty, the enjoyment of others' suffering, or with endless fears, worries, lies, obsessions, meannesses and betrayals, the effect of the compression of these images would be terrible beyond any hell describable by man.

To live one's life in forty minutes would mean that all perceptions and feelings would be compressed or heightened a millionfold. 'The bitterness of pain that we now feel in one hour seemeth as great as all the sorrows of the passing world in a hundred years', as the dying cry in the mediaeval 'Orologium Sapientiae'.* The hates of years would be compressed into the hate of minutes, but a million times more intense; the joys of aspiration, of discovery, of affection, heightened a millionfold, would become god-like ecstasies.

Moreover, by the compression of time, such hates or cruelties would not only be heightened beyond bearing, but would be experienced *together* with all the fear, resentment and suffering to which they gave rise, and whose connection is normally hidden by the merciful oblivion of expanded time. While, on the other hand, such aspiration and devotion would become *joined* to the perceptions of higher laws and higher worlds towards which they led. *This would indeed be to ascend to heaven and descend to hell.*

* *The Book of the Craft of Dying*, edited by F. M. M. Comper, p. 119

III

THE SOUL
IN THE MOLECULAR WORLD

WE must try to study the true meaning of the three circles round which the individual self passes in its total career through life and death. Hitherto we imagined these circles as successive in time—the familiar circle consisting of seventy-six years' existence in the physical world of cellular organisms; before that the circle of a month's existence in a non-physical world, where all phenomena are a thousand times intensified and compressed; and before that again yet another circle of existence, lasting but forty minutes, where all is a million times faster than in physical life.

Yet the idea of these states as *successive* comes only from man's nature. In fact, they represent *different worlds* in which an individual man spends these fixed periods. And just as the cellular world of nature continues to exist whether any given individual is alive and participating in it or not, so these other worlds must be ever present, even though a man can expect such brief taste of them. The periods seventy-six years, one month, and forty minutes are those which the mechanism of man is designed to pass in each of these three worlds, as this same mechanism is designed to pass ten months in the womb, seven years in childhood, and seventy in bodily maturity. Put in another way, these periods mark the time which the original impulse of an individual life, the quantum of energy assigned by higher laws to each human atom, takes to overcome the varying resistances set up by the three media—just as a bullet shot from a rifle must pass through wood at one speed, through water at another, and through air at a third.

What then is the nature of these three worlds? The world of organic life in which the physical body of man spends seventy-six years is familiar enough. Its chief characteristic is cellular structure, and its processes are determined by the lifetime and speed of reaction of cells. But as we agreed in the last chapter, the time-scale of man, appearing to run faster and faster as we look back towards birth and beyond, at conception disappears out of the world of nature altogether. Any increase of speed beyond that ruling at conception cannot be contained within a cellular body. The lifetime and speed of reaction of cells are too slow for it.

Therefore if the career of man does continue to accelerate beyond conception it must do so in a finer world than that of cellular organisms. This world is the world of molecular ones.

As is well known, matter in a molecular form enjoys far greater freedom than matter in cellular form. The properties of matter in molecular form can be well studied in scents and smells. Such matter enjoys extraordinary powers of duration, penetration, and diffusion, without change of its own nature. A grain or two of musk will scent an apartment for years, at the end of which time no appreciable loss of weight can be detected. The same perfume can pass through a cotton-wool filter which eliminates all particles larger than a hundred-thousandth of an inch in size. Mercaptan can be recognized, that is to say, it retains its nature, even when diluted in fifty million million times its own volume of air.*

Thus while cellular bodies can travel only along a *line*, and in man's case normally at no greater speed than a few miles an hour, scents can diffuse a hundred times as fast, and in all plane directions at once, that is over an *area*. This area may be unbelievably vast in relation to their original concentrated form. In fact, the only comparable expansion to be found in the cellular world lies not in movement at all, but in *growth*, the human organism, for example, increasing its

* *Encyclopaedia Britannica* (14th ed.), 'Smell and Taste' by G. H. Parker

own volume 250 million times between conception and maturity. But such cellular expansion requires years to produce what molecular diffusion achieves in minutes; that is to say, growth in the molecular world, if we may call it that, is hundreds of thousands of times faster than in the cellular world—just as we should expect it to be from our logarithmic scale.

Again, no cellular body can occupy the same space as another cellular body. But two scents can occupy the same space. And the scent of one cellular body can occupy the same space as another cellular body; that is, the scent can permeate it, as milk left in the refrigerator with an onion becomes permeated with the latter's odour.

Imagine human consciousness endowed with the properties of matter in such molecular state. It could then perform many of the miracles ascribed to magicians and would in fact possess the capacities often attributed to the soul after death. It could be present in many places simultaneously, it could pass through walls, it could assume different shapes, it could enter *inside* other men, be aware of what was happening in their various organs, and so on. Like the musk, it might 'haunt' a place for years; and were a molecular body of human size endowed with the pungency of mercaptan it could make its influence felt over an area equivalent to half a continent.

Now consider the words addressed to the dead person in the *Tibetan Book of the Dead:*

O nobly-born . . . thy present body being a desire body . . . is not a body of gross matter, so that now thou hast the power to go right through any rock-masses, hills, boulders, earth, houses, and Mount Meru itself without being impeded. . . . Thou art actually endowed with the power of miraculous action, which is not however the fruit of any samadhi, but a power come to thee naturally. . . . Thou canst instantaneously arrive in whatever place thou wishest; thou hast the power of reaching there within the time which a man taketh to bend, or to stretch forth his hand. These various powers of illusion and of shape-shifting desire not, desire not.*

* W. Y. Evans-Wentz: *The Tibetan Book of the Dead*, pp. 158-9 (O.U.P.)

The powers here described are those belonging to matter in a molecular state, and the so-called 'desire-body', or *soul*, as we should rather call it, is composed of such matter, just as the physical body is composed of cellular matter.

This idea is curiously supported by the immemorial custom, particularly important in Tibetan,* Egyptian† and Peruvian rituals, of setting aside fresh food and drink from the smell or essence of which the soul of the dead man is supposed to derive its nourishment. Here is a clear recognition of the fact that the physical nature of the soul is similar to that of scent, that is, it consists of matter in a molecular state.

The second circle then, in which the individual self passes one month, appears to represent the world of molecular phenomena. This world, of course, pervades or permeates the cellular world of nature. But man cannot enjoy the powers belonging to molecular matter so long as his consciousness is locked in a cellular or physical body. At the death of this physical body, however, the texts suggest that a new body, apparently of molecular matter, is born, and that this enjoys a complete existence and acts as the vehicle of human consciousness in the interval before the individuality is ready to be conceived into a new physical body.

In ordinary man, the molecular body or soul seems to be born, to grow, achieve maturity and expire all within its month's term, in exactly the same way as does the physical body in its seventy-six years. This idea is expressed with startling exactness in a Zoroastrian text, the 'Rivayat of Shahpur Baruchi':

> On the first day (after death) the size of the soul is like that of a newly born infant. On the second day the soul grows to the size of a child at the age of seven. On the third day the size of the soul becomes as that of an adult at the age of fifteen.‡

* W. Y. Evans-Wentz: *The Tibetan Book of the Dead*, p. 19
† Sir E. A. Wallis Budge: *The Book of the Dead*, pp. 242-3, etc. Note also the phrase: 'I know also the great god before whose *nostrils* ye place celestial food', p. 301
‡ Rivayat of Darab Hormazdyar, vol. 1, p. 147, quoted by J. D. C. Pavry, *The Zoroastrian Doctrine of a Future Life*, p. 20

If we place on one circle the parallel times of the body and of the soul according to our logarithmic scale, their correspondence with the Zoroastrian calculation is remarkable. On this scale the soul at one day corresponds to an infant of about two years, at two days to a child of five, while something over five of its days are equivalent to physical puberty.

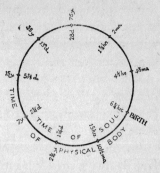

This parallel between the infancy, childhood and maturity of the soul and that of the body, seems in another aspect to connect with the idea expressed in the *Tibetan Book of the Dead* that in the first seven days of the soul's journey it encounters the Peaceful Deities and in the next seven the Wrathful ones, or with St. Makary's account of six days passed in paradise and then thirty in hell. For in the physical life of the body, infancy and childhood may also be seen as a period corresponding to paradise, and advancing age to plunge the individual deeper and deeper into a realization of the tragedy, fear and suffering of the world in which he lives.

In the same way, individual consciousness born into the world of molecular phenomena might at first tend to be overwhelmed by the miraculousness and beauty of the new perceptions and powers with which it was endowed. But then gradually as its limited time drew towards a close it could be expected to become obsessed with the terrible aspect even of that world, and with forebodings as to its own future state. For wherever time and change exist, no matter what the scale of such time, successive states corresponding to spring, summer, autumn, winter; to dawn, day, evening, night; to infancy, childhood, maturity and old age, must inevitably be found. And the world of the soul, being equally subject to time and change, could be no exception.

C

Yet it must be remembered that beings in such a world would exist in one more dimension than beings endowed with cellular bodies. The capacity of movement in all directions simultaneously, that is, of moving over areas instead of over lines, has already been mentioned. So also, that of penetration into and through solid objects. Both these capacities are merely isolated effects of freedom in another dimension.

Put in a general way, we may say that cellular bodies are free to move throughout the world of other cellular matter. This means, in principle, that physical men are free within the *world of nature*, which covers the whole surface of the earth. But molecular bodies, in the same general way, would be free to move throughout the world of molecular matter, that is, throughout the whole solid sphere of rock, soil, water and air which comprises the *world of earth*. For all this is of molecular structure. This possibility, which is clearly indicated in the Tibetan text already quoted, is of course only a theoretical one, for just as individual men in their physical bodies, although free in principle to travel over the whole surface of the earth, may in fact pass their whole lives within a few miles of their birthplace, so probably would their souls remain equally incurious after death.

Such freedom would also make literally possible the universal idea that the souls of the righteous pass *upwards*, to a paradise which by all the legends and hints appears to exist in the upper reaches of the atmosphere. And it would also throw light on our own earlier deduction of a certain affinity between true man (that is, the soul which distinguishes him from other vertebrate animals) and the ionosphere which lies sixty miles above the surface of the earth.*

But for the moment we must content ourselves with the general idea, deduced from our logarithmic time-scale, that the souls of men after death may exist in a molecular world, and in such condition would enjoy freedom of another dimension beyond those available to man in the cellular

* *The Theory of Celestial Influence*, chapters 7 and 8

body of physical life. And further, that the powers, capacities and sensations belonging to such molecular state would correspond very closely with those which from time immemorial and in all parts of the world have been attributed to the souls of the dead.

If, moreover, we combine all that follows from this power of penetration of molecular matter, with the effects of the compression of time discussed in the last chapter, we shall see that the state of the soul in a molecular world must be utterly unimaginable to men whose awareness is locked into the slow and rigid form of a cellular body. And that to a consciousness enjoying the freedom of that other state confinement within a physical body, if it could be conceived, would have all the terror of solitary confinement in a dark, cold and narrow-windowed dungeon.

A very vivid description of this idea is given in the oldest Hermetic writing, the 'Kore Kosmu':

Then first did the souls learn that they were sentenced; and gloomy were their looks. . . . When they were about to be shut up in the bodies, some of them wailed and moaned, just that and nothing more; but some there were that struggled against their doom, even as beasts of noble temper, when they are caught by the crafty tricks of cruel men, and dragged away from the wild land that is their home, strive to fight against those who have mastered them. And another shrieked, and again and again turning his eyes now upward and now downward, said, 'O thou Heaven, source of our being, and ye bright-shining stars, and never-failing light of sun and moon; and ye, aether and air, and holy life-breath of Him who rules alone, ye that have shared our home; how cruel it is that we are being torn away from things so great and splendid! . . .

'We are to be expelled from the holy atmosphere and a place nigh to the vault of heaven, and from the blissful life we lived there, and to be imprisoned in habitations mean and base as these. . . . What hateful things we shall have to do, in order to supply the needs of this body that must so soon perish! Our eyes will have little room to take things in; we shall see things only by means of the fluid which these orbs contain; and when we see Heaven, our own forefather, contracted to small compass, we shall never cease to moan. And even if we see, we shall not see outright; for alas, we have been condemned to darkness. And when we hear the winds, our kinsmen, blowing in the air, deeply shall we grieve that we are not breathing in unison with them. For dwelling-place, instead of this world on high, there awaits us a man's heart, a thing of little bulk. Unhappy we! What have we done to deserve such punishments as these?'*

Apart from the tremendous emotional force of the writing, we are struck by the number of references to the condition which the souls are leaving as a *gaseous* or *molecular* state. 'Ye, *aether* and *air*, and holy life-*breath* of Him who rules alone. . . . We are to be expelled from the holy *atmosphere*, and a place nigh to the vault of heaven . . . and when we hear the *winds*, our kinsmen, blowing in the *air*, deeply shall we grieve that we are not *breathing* in unison with them . . .' Air, atmosphere, breath is matter in a molecular state, and the whole passage seems to be striving to convey the anguish of a consciousness transferred from a molecular body to the confines of a cellular one. Particularly striking is the idea of the narrowing of perception which on a molecular level would *embrace* objects, but on a cellular one sees them from a single angle, minified by perspective, and then 'only by means of the fluid which these orbs contain', rather than by direct contact and penetration.

This passage emphasizes with great poignancy the idea that the experiences of the soul belong to *the true world*, a world which is always there, but from which men are exiled while in the physical body. Poetic as this may sound, there could be no more exact description of the relation between the matters appropriate to each. We know scientifically enough that the molecular world *permeates* the cellular one, and that the electronic world *permeates* the molecular one. These three worlds are always co-existent. But whereas the finer worlds can penetrate the coarser, as light can penetrate glass, or smells can penetrate butter or milk, objects of the coarser structure have no way of entering into the finer. They are excluded as clearly as was the camel from passing through the eye of a needle.

* From the 'Kore Kosmu' included in *Hermetica*, edited by Walter Scott, pp. 475-7

And yet if those worlds are ever-present, and pervade every living creature at every moment, and if life in them is so infinitely more free, wonderful, awesome and illuminated than that with which we are familiar, we cannot but hanker after the impossible, and demand whether there is not in fact a way leading from our physical world to those, which may be trodden even before death.

Only such a longing can lead us to understand correctly the hard saying that ordinary man during physical life has no conscious soul, and why the creation of such a soul in this life is the greatest task he can possibly attempt. For the soul is man's vehicle in the invisible or molecular world. From all that has gone before, it is indisputable that man does not now live in such a world, and cannot even imagine what it would be like to do so. Either his soul is not yet born, as the texts suggest, or if it does exist somewhere then he does not yet yet know how to live in it.

Imagine a locked greenhouse. A seed is introduced through the crack of the door and planted. It germinates, buds, and grows to full flower. In this form it is confined to the locked room and cannot possibly pass into the world outside. When the flower turns to fruit, produces new seed, and itself dies, then such seed may pass out again through the door-chink. This is a natural cycle. In its 'expanded' form, however, the flower has only one possibility of communication with the world beyond the door—its *scent*, if it has any, may pass freely through the crack to what lies beyond, even though the cellular plant remain confined to the end of its existence.

This process appears to bear an exact analogy to the entrance of man into the physical world, his growth there, and his departure elsewhere. The seed of men appears to emerge from the molecular world. But the cellular body which grows from it is absolutely confined here, and if man is nothing but physical body he can have no communication with his invisible world of origin, until death again reduces him to an essential form sufficiently condensed to pass there.

Only if he can develop in himself now something analogous to scent in the flower, that is, *a soul or principle of consciousness*, can he begin to move in that other world while yet alive in this.

How could this be? The soul, or body of the molecular world, can only be created artificially by long accumulation of the finest energy which the physical organism produces, and its crystallization through the continuous attempt to become self-conscious. But ordinary man *cannot help* spending this energy as fast as it is produced—on fear, anger, envy, longing, and his normal state of fascination with himself and the world round him. In order to restrain this wasting of it, he must create *will* in himself. In order to create will he must have *one aim*. In order to have one aim he must have learned all sides of himself, and forced them to accept the domination of his *conscience*. Before this he must first awake conscience from sleep. And not one of these stages can he achieve by himself.

Yet the possibility exists—and carries with it immense implications, not only for man's situation now, but also afterwards. It is this possibility alone which justifies our study.

IV

THE SPIRIT
IN THE ELECTRONIC WORLD

DESPITE the wonders of such an existence as we have deduced, there is much that is still unexplained. At the end of the second circle forty minutes yet remain. Looking back even beyond the birth of the soul, to a point where the equivalent of a lifetime is compressed into this short hour, we shall find phenomena transcending even the molecular world, just as they passed out of the cellular one beyond conception. The third circle, in which the individual self appears to live a full career in forty minutes, must exist in an even faster and finer world than the molecular one. This is the electronic world.

By analogy the vehicle which the self inhabited in this circle and this world would be constituted of matter in its electronic state. Our chief example of matter in this state is light. And if molecular energy such as scent or sound diffuses a hundred times faster than cellular bodies move, light radiates nearly a million times faster still.* Light travels instantaneously in three dimensions, that is, not only along a *line* like a cellular body, nor over an *area*, like a smell, but throughout a *volume* of space. In principle, being independent of atmosphere, it can travel indefinitely upwards beyond the earth's influence, and in seven minutes reach the very source of all our light, the sun itself.

Further, light or matter in such electronic state itself illuminates everything upon which it falls, the higher degrees

---

* Speed of man (average)   3 metres per second (6 m.p.h.)
  Speed of sound   300 metres per second
  Speed of light   300,000 kilometres per second

of electronic matter, such as X-rays, even having the property of illuminating the *interior* of solid objects. A body of such matter would thus be its own illuminant, and in its perception would be independent of the illumination of the sun, the moon or other ordinary sources of light. It would perceive wherever it was, by its own power of diffusion and penetration, and this perception could embrace both the largest and smallest objects, as the *same light* can illuminate at the same time a large room and a cell under a microscope in that room.

Try to imagine human consciousness attached to the light of a bright electric lamp in a room, and conveyed wherever its radiations penetrate. The electronic body enjoyed by such a consciousness would have its focus or heart, so to speak, in the white-hot filament of the lamp, but would include *all the light* emitted by this source. If the lamp produced an equal diffusion of light, then the consciousness so endowed would embrace *within itself* all the objects in the room, whether tables, chairs, flowers or men and women. In this way, it would illuminate or be aware of each object *from all sides simultaneously*. All such objects would become as it were inner organs of this electronic body, and would be realized as with ordinary senses we realize organs and sensations inside the physical body. In this latter case, we know that the pain or joy of the heart is *our* pain or joy, the motions arising in the brain are *our* thoughts, the sensations of well-being or discomfort produced by the processes of digestion in the stomach are *our* sensations. So, to a consciousness attached to the light of this electric lamp, everything happening in the room would be happening inside it, and would be sensed *as its own life*.

This exactly corresponds, though in a small way, to what is described in many theologies as the nature of God, *in whom all creatures exist and have their being*. Human consciousness attached to a body of electronic matter would include all neighbouring beings in itself, and would thus share the nature of God, be *joined* both to God and to them. This is evidently the significance both of yoga which means 'union', and of religion which means 're-union'.

We can even think further about the functions of such a body. If we suppose the lamp to be one of the widest possible range of radiation, then its lowest function would be infra-red radiation or heat, its middle functions would be represented by light of various colours, red, yellow, green and blue, its higher functions by ultra-violet and X-rays. Its functions would thus be to impart to other creatures warmth, colour, and growth, while with its highest frequencies it would be able to penetrate and sustain all their inward parts. It would in fact be life-giving.

Further, if cellular bodies are in principle free of the cellular world of nature, and molecular bodies free of the molecular world of the earth, by analogy electronic bodies would be free of the electronic world. That is to say, they could exist or travel wherever electronic matter is found, just as physical man can exist or travel anywhere on the earth's surface, where other cellular matter is found. But the sun's radiation is electronic matter, and this radiation fills the whole solar system. So that such an electronic body by its nature should be free of the whole solar system. It would partake of the nature of the sun. Such a body we call *spirit*.

Now if our deductions from the logarithmic scale are correct, man's individuality, which inhabits a physical body for seventy-six years, has previously inhabited a soul for one month, and before that a spirit for forty minutes. And birth into that spirit was simultaneous with the death of the previous physical body. In other words, at the instant of death man enters the electronic world or world of the spirit.

From what we have guessed of the nature of experience in the electronic world, we can see that this forty minutes of experience in the spirit could in fact be described by St. Makary's words: 'On the third day Christ commands every Christian soul to ascend to heaven for adoration of the

Almighty God.' It is during this period that the dead man is addressed in the *Tibetan Book of the Dead* as follows:

O nobly-born, listen. Now thou art experiencing the Radiance of the Clear Light of Pure Reality. Recognize it. O nobly-born, thy present intellect, in real nature void, not formed into anything as regards characteristics or colour, naturally void, is the very reality, the All-Good.

Thine own intellect, which is now voidness, yet not to be regarded as of the voidness of nothingness, but as being the intellect itself, unobstructed, shining, thrilling and blissful, is the very consciousness, the All-Good Buddha.

Thine own consciousness, shining, void and inseparable from the Great Body of Radiance, hath no birth, nor death, and is the Immutable Light—Buddha Amitabha.*

Such experience, inexpressible in any language or ideas available to physical man, must necessarily be translated into terms of the philosophy with which those so illuminated are familiar. The Christian St. Makary 'ascends to Heaven for adoration of the Almighty God'; the Buddhist lama becomes 'inseparable from the Great Body of Radiance'. And we, making our deductions in present-day scientific terms, seem to see that this can mean nothing else but becoming free of the whole solar system and ascending to the very source of electronic energy, which is the sun.

'To become free of the solar system'—how is such an experience conceivable? Here the vision of Er the Pamphylian returns to mind. For the souls with whom Er journeyed came to a place where they could see a

Straight Light extended from above through the whole Heaven and Earth, as it were a pillar, for colour like unto the rainbow, but brighter and purer. . . . This Light is that which bindeth the Heavens together; as the undergirths hold together ships so doth it hold together the whole round of Heaven; and from the ends extendeth the Spindle of Necessity, which causeth all the heavenly revolutions.†

* W. Y. Evans-Wentz: *The Tibetan Book of the Dead*, pp. 95-6 (Book 1, Part 1, 'The Bardo of the Moments of Death')—Buddha Amitabha: in Sanskrit and Tibetan, 'The Buddha of Infinite Light'; in Mongolian, 'He who is eternally brilliant'; in another aspect, Amitayus, 'The Buddha of Eternal Life'. A. Getty: *The Gods of Northern Buddhism*, p. 37.

† *The Myths of Plato*, trs. by J. A. Stewart, p. 141

The whorl of this spindle contained within itself seven other whorls set one within the other, like caskets, upon each of which was mounted a Siren uttering a note at one pitch, all the notes together making a single harmony. While seated on thrones nearby were the three Fates, of past, present and future, who spun the whorls, one forward, one backward, and the third alternately one way and the other. And the great Shaft of Light passed down through the centre of all.

We now see that this represents an *actual perception* of that which, in another book,* we so laboriously and theoretically deduced—the long body of the solar system, the unimaginably glorious shaft of the four-dimensional sun sheathed in the singing spirals of the planetary orbits and in which the eighty years of man's life *exist together* in a single moment. This is the electronic world—of which the spirit is a free citizen, and into which the being of man appears to be born for the timeless forty minutes after death.

So also perceived St. John in Patmos:

I was in the Spirit on the Lord's day, and heard behind me a great voice, as of a trumpet, saying, I am Alpha and Omega, the first and the last. . . .
And I turned to see the voice that spake with me. And being turned, I saw seven golden candlesticks; and in the midst of the seven candlesticks one like unto the Son of man, clothed with a garment down to the foot, and girt about the paps with a golden girdle. His head and his hairs were white like wool, as white as snow; and his eyes were as a flame of fire; and his feet like unto fine brass, as if they burned in a furnace; and his voice as the sound of many waters. And he had in his right hand seven stars: and out of his mouth went a sharp two-edged sword: and his countenance was as the sun shineth in his strength. . . .
And he laid his right hand upon me, saying, Fear not; I am the first and the last: I am he that liveth, and was dead; and, behold, I am alive for evermore, Amen; and have the keys of hell and death.†

This is the same vision of the *being of the solar system*, its countenance the sun amid the seven lights of the planets,

* *The Theory of Celestial Influence*, chapter 3
† *The Revelation of St. John the Divine*, 1, 10-18

its body clothed with their sheaths, and adorned with the sword of Mars, the girdle of Venus, the halo of Saturn, and feet of shining Mercury. Such a vision can only be that of a consciousness endowed with an electronic body and existing in the electronic world, where, as we said, it would be free of the whole solar system. 'I was in the Spirit. . . .' as John himself declares.

Yet by this very description St. John answers our earlier question. For, unlike Er the Pamphylian, John did not apparently have to enter the gates of death to see such a vision. According to his testimony, he was 'in the Spirit', that is, he had entered the electronic world, and through its medium saw the whole eternal being of the solar system, *while still physically alive*. Furthermore, he returned to our world and even endeavoured to write down what he had experienced, though the task was obviously impossible.

Such a man must have acquired for himself, in this very life, not only a soul but a spirit. As Noah spent his days making an ark with which to survive in the coming world of water, these in their time on earth achieved a vehicle with which to ride the electronic cataclysm and survive in a world of light. But whereas Noah's task was to create an extra and yet harder shell for human consciousness, these had to transfer consciousness to a new vehicle not only far finer than the physical body, but *finer than any existing energy within it*.

What does this mean? Though we neither understand nor dream what it may require to make a soul, this creation of a new body with materials which are available but wasted, is at least imaginable. The spirit, however, is made of materials which are *not available*. For man does not ordinarily dispose of free electronic energy. He does not emit light. He cannot normally transmit his thoughts or perform actions at a distance. He enjoys no power characteristic of this state of matter. He may be said to have *right* to a soul, even though he has not got one; but to a spirit he has *no natural right*. His spirit was a free gift from God in the beginning, and remains with Him. To find it man must return whence he came.

The achievement of spirit implies *transmutation of matter*. A man has first to acquire a soul by diverting all his molecular energy to this one end. Then he has to learn how to connect this soul with a still higher level—a level at which *it cannot be misused*. He must transmute it to an intensity which individual personality cannot survive and where understanding is therefore permanent. Such intensity is found only on the electronic level. This means he must infuse soul with spirit. In himself he has to learn how to convert molecular matter into electronic, that is, to split the atom and release *internally* a degree of energy which only our own age can begin to measure. It is the release of such energy which alone can carry him up into that divine world attested by these visions.

All this means that *we cannot imagine* the achievement of spirit. We can only say that John's record, even if it conveys little, proves the most important thing of all—that a way does exist from the physical world of living men to the electronic or divine world, and that actual men have both passed there and returned.

V

MAN'S BEING
IN THE INVISIBLE WORLDS

HAVING dimly perceived the unlimited possibilities of the molecular and electronic worlds through which man appears to pass between death and birth, there is one fundamental idea which we must now face. This is the idea that man's *powers* and his *being* are two quite different things, and that the use he makes of the former must always depend upon the latter.

It is generally accepted that a strong man is not necessarily a good man. He may be or he may not be. There is no connection between the two characteristics. His strength belongs to his *powers*, his degree of goodness to his *being*. And he may use this strength equally to labour for those weaker than himself, or to force them to labour for him.

We can see the same thing in cases of temporary acquisition of new powers. It may sometimes happen that a man releases in himself some source of almost superhuman energy and endurance, when for a short time he can do the impossible and is unaffected by danger, pain, or ordinary considerations of safety or fear. But in one man's case this power may be released say in the rescue of a child from a burning house, while for another man it is connected with an access of blind rage in which he runs wild, attacking with a knife everyone he may meet. The energy may be similar, but it is at the service of *different being*.

In the same way the sudden inheritance of a great fortune may bring all kinds of new and interesting possibilities to a thoughtful and self-controlled man, while a weak man will be destroyed by the flood of new temptations which he is unable to master. Increase of power always involves a crucial *test* of the vehicle, as increased electrical voltage will cause one lamp to shine with doubled brilliance while another is instantly burnt out. This may be said to be a test of the being of the two lamps.

It is a fundamental idea that change to a new state does not imply a change in man's being; but on the contrary the true being of the man will be then revealed, no matter how well he may have concealed it before. This has always been recognized in occult thought, in which *black magic* was often taken to represent the acquisition of new powers, where the being of the man, with all its weaknesses, desires, and personal lusts and ambitions remained the same. The Tarot card of the Chariot refers to the same thing, as also the legend of Icarus who flew too near the sun with wings attached only by wax and, this melting in the heat, was thrown headlong to destruction. 'Wings' are evidently new powers and 'wax' old weaknesses.

Entry into the electronic and molecular worlds at death, with all that that implies, must thus be the last and most terrible test of man's being.

How can a man judge his own being? His being is measured by his desires, by what he wants. This is the method traditionally used in fairy-tales, where the man to be tested by fate is given three wishes. And as such tales show, man's wishes are usually so impulsive, contradictory and destructive, that by the time he reaches the third he can usually do no more than wish himself back in the circumstances he enjoyed at the beginning, and out of the appalling difficulties he has created by the first two.

There is a strange echo here of the three successive lives of man—in spirit, soul, and body—and a hint of why, after being presented with the miraculous possibilities of the first two, he may, as the Myth of Er suggests, be able to think of nothing better than to choose the identical example of a physical life which was his before.

If we want to judge man's being from the point of view of the ultimate test of death, the first question will be—to what

world do his desires refer? For desires referring to the
physical or cellular world will naturally be as out of place
and dangerous there, as the infantile desire to be suckled
would be in the world of grown-up men. What could happen to a man whose whole being is made up of desires connected with physical comfort, the sensations of food and
drink, and the purely physical side of sex, if he has no cellular body and does not exist in a cellular world? He will be
like a fish out of water, for whom the fact that the possibilities of existence in air are infinitely greater means nothing
at all: every moment there will be agony for him, and he
can only long with all his being to be thrown back into the
sea.

The impact of such a change of state on a person who is
completely unprepared for it, and whose whole being has
been centred on physical phenomena, would inevitably produce unconsciousness, just as a man who had been locked in
a dark cell for years, and was then suddenly driven out into
bright sunlight, would be utterly blinded and would probably faint. The *Tibetan Book of the Dead*, indeed, emphasizes that all ordinary men are thrown at death into a swoon
which lasts three and a half days; that is, according to our
logarithmic scale, throughout the whole life of the spirit
spent in the electronic world, and through two-thirds of the
life of the soul in the molecular one. Such finer states of
matter, with all their miraculous possibilities of knowing,
penetrating and understanding, according to this idea are *too
strong* for unprepared men, who only recover from their
swoon in the old age of the soul when processes have already slowed down to a speed only ten times faster than at
conception.

According to the same text, to the *Egyptian Book of the
Dead*, the mediaeval *Book of the Craft of Dying*, and other
such teachings, intense preparation must be undergone by
the dying man to make him able to *bear* the intense shock of
new states. The quicker he can regain consciousness the
higher will he be able to ascend and the more understand

and experience. Like a man diving into an ice-cold sea, there is bound to be a momentary blackout of awareness, but all depends on how quickly he can recover and remember himself.

Thus if the *Tibetan Book of the Dead* may be taken as probable, most unprepared men would never experience the life of the spirit, or the electronic world at all, even though by the arrangement of the universe, each man is *entitled* to do so. It is his deathright, which he sells for the mess of pottage of material attachments.

In the ordinary state of his being it cannot be otherwise. Passage from the physical world into the molecular world may be compared with the explosion of a bomb, the constituents of which in one moment change from a few cubic inches of gelatine into thousands of cubic feet of gas. But passage from the physical world into the electronic world would be literally akin to the detonation of an atom bomb, the expansion being so great that a vortex was created right through the earth's atmosphere and out into solar space. Pictures of the atomic explosion, indeed, illustrate in a very startling way the idea of 'ascending into heaven'.

But what man's consciousness is strong enough to become attached to the explosion of an atomic bomb and retain its awareness? When irritation or flattery or a sudden shout may instantly deprive men of all sense of their own individual presence and existence, what possibility is there of them retaining such a sense through the unimaginable shock of death?

For that a man would have to be most intensely prepared and trained. He would have to acquire an incredibly strong being, which by superhuman efforts had become accustomed to withstand, without loss of self-consciousness, the most intense shocks, hardships, deprivations and violences which can be met with in the physical world. Only then could he hope to bear the final shock of death without swooning into insensibility.

Such a possibility clearly does not refer to ordinary man.

D

The latter's problem in death will be how to orientate him-self, where to turn for support when, as addressed in the vivid words of the *Tibetan Book of the Dead*,

thou hast been in a swoon during the last three and one-half days. As soon as thou art recovered from this swoon, thou wilt have the thought, 'What hath happened!' [For] at that time all the Sangsara [phenomenal universe] will be in revolution.*

We may therefore try to imagine the sensations of a man awaking into the molecular world, and ask how this awaken-ing would be affected by the nature of his being.

His first problem would of course refer to himself. What has happened to me? And here at once his sensation or re-action would depend upon his attitude towards himself during life. For most people, the idea of *themselves* is con-nected with a body of a certain age, shape, and degree of health, containing certain physical sensations and recurrent pains, and labelled with a certain name. To such people, the sensation of being deprived of this body would be one of the greatest horror. They would not know who they were, or if they existed at all. Anyone who has felt, when their intimate association with the body was shaken by the effect of anaesthetics or by some profound emotional shock, the extraordinary sensation: 'Who am I? Do I really exist?' will already have a dim foretaste of such an experience.

To a man of weak or fearful being, this sense of having no body and thus not existing, would give rise to the most pro-found terror. And he would immediately endeavour to create or imagine for himself a body like that which he was accustomed to call 'I'. Since he would be existing in a molecu-lar world, and endowed with a body of molecular matter, which by its nature could pass anywhere or take any form, he would desperately try to shape this into a semblance of his old physical body. The more firmly his individuality was identified with his body in life, the better he might be ex-pected to succeed in this: and such is the responsiveness of molecular matter to thought that he might even persuade

* W. Y. Evans-Wentz: *The Tibetan Book of the Dead*, p. 105

himself that he still possessed his old body, or had never even left it.

In this way everything might still seem familiar; he would be reassured that *he did exist*. Yet by the very same token he would have voluntarily sacrificed all the new experiences and opportunities of different perception and understanding inherent in the world in which he now lived.

For example, his molecular body, as we concluded earlier, would have the power of pervading other physical bodies and thus sensing their nature: it could become aware of the essence of another man, or of a tree or a rock. The molecular body would thus have an enormously increased power of understanding the nature of the universe, and of becoming one with other creatures. But the man of weak being would be terrified of any such experiment, which for him would mean the loss of his physical shape and identity, without which he would have no confirmation of his existence.

It now becomes clear why the electronic world is mercifully closed by swoon to ordinary men. For though one might make oneself a shadow of a physical identity in the molecular world, out of a stuff comparable to scent, in the electronic world such an endeavour would be quite impossible. The tremendous speed, brilliance and power of diffusion of the energy involved, would mean that at every second individuality would collapse into an abyss of light and force; and any attempt to keep it so confined would be a thousand times more futile than trying to carve a statue out of quicksilver. In such a world, the man who could not transcend ordinary ideas of 'physical self', would go mad with terror and frustration, were he not saved by insensibility, just as in life he is saved by fainting from too much pain.

In the molecular world, on the other hand, we *can* conceive of the circumstances, surroundings, illusions and habits of physical life being simulated, and even acquiring a spurious kind of existence, though divorced from the cellular bodies which alone gave them meaning. Since the being of man does not change with state, those cravings which obsessed a man's being in the physical world, whether for riches, comfort, women, food or drink, would still obsess him there; and having no means of enjoying the physical objects of his desire, he would have to content himself with the molecular 'scents' or essences emitted by them.

A curious story is told by W. Y. Evans-Wentz, of native villagers in South-west India ritualistically pouring special brands of beer and whisky over the grave of a dead European planter, whose ghost, they declared, would not leave them in peace until supplied with the same beverages he required in life.* In the same way, such obsessed souls could be expected to haunt the places or people which had most intensely attracted their physical craving.

What physical craving is to the body, unlicensed imagination is to the mind. This also is a chief index of man's being. What then would be the role of imagination in the molecular world of the soul? In the material world, a man's dreams of rosy or horrid possibilities are always limited sooner or later by the facts of physical existence, the necessity of providing food and shelter for a physical body or physical dependents. Here he must sometimes emerge from his dreams, if only to eat or avoid being run over. But in the immaterial world—unhampered by actuality—he could live *entirely* in dreams. He could pass his whole time amid the scenes and circumstances created by his own imagination, playing there his favourite imaginary rôles, with no more interruption than that provided by the equally imaginary fears and terrors arising from other sides of his own mind. Such imaginary scenery, adventures and characters would naturally depend on the experience, longings and apprehensions of the man in life, and they would be different for each individual. In the *Tibetan Book of the Dead*, for example, extremely complicated and detailed visions of gods, demons, heavens and hells are described for each day after death, but always with the admonition to the dead man:

* W. Y. Evans-Wentz: *The Tibetan Book of the Dead*, p. xxxv

'Fear that not. Be not terrified. Be not awed. Recognize them to be the embodiment of thine own intellect.'*

Thus while each man could in the molecular world experience his own heaven and his own hell, all this would have no objective reality. He would live only amid the *shadows* of real things, unable, like Tantalus, ever to touch or taste the grapes whose image hung before him. Such would be the lot of men of purely physical nature in a non-physical world. These are the shadowy dead of the Greek Hades, the unhappy ghosts of the Tibetan Pretaloka, doting upon what they can never enjoy.

At the same time, we must remember the principle that ordinary unprepared men can never judge the being, or assess the inner values and real attachments of other men, because their own habits and prejudices inevitably stand in the way. Thus it may happen that some men who *appear* to us entirely devoted to physical sensation may actually have turned in this direction from disillusionment with the more artificial sides of human life; or again, through growth of awareness they may have discovered a way to make physical impressions feed both the mental and emotional sides of their nature as well. Evidently the lot of such men in the invisible world might be very different from what has been described.

For one factor only would separate the purgatory suffered by the brutally sensual, from an unimaginable paradise of new knowledge, freedom, experience and truth. That factor is the difference between the cravings and longings of men of different being.

For even as from men of physical appetite death takes away their sole means of indulgence, from men of unselfish and nobler impulse it would remove their chief obstacle and present unbelievable opportunity of satisfying such aspiration. The man who longed for knowledge, and who in such interest could forget personal desires and weaknesses, would in his new state be enabled to understand by direct perception the working of natural laws. His molecular struc-

* W. Y. Evans-Wentz: *The Tibetan Book of the Dead*, p. 141

ture, for example, would enable him to *perceive* the nature of magnetism, of sound and music, and so on; he might expand his awareness to comprehend the being of mountains, seas and other organic unities too big to be embraced by the physical senses. And since the lowest limit of physical sight and physical touch, operating through their cellular instruments, is an object of the scale of largest cells, so the perceptions of a molecular body might be expected to penetrate down into the realm of individual molecules.

A body of molecular matter and endowed with human intelligence would be itself microscope and telescope, as well as an instrument for many other kinds of super-physical sensation not yet simulated by man-made mechanisms. A scientist so endowed, if not frustrated by purely human fears and weaknesses, would certainly exist in his own particular kind of paradise.

The poet also, relying in the physical world on vague presentiments of emotions, scenes and moods, on indefinable sensations of the being of men, women, cities, seas and forests, could there perceive the nature of such things directly, by *penetration* rather than external perception. The philanthropist would at last be able to understand the needs of others, instead of imposing his own upon them. While the man desiring to learn would be enabled to pass momentarily across the world in search of a teacher of the level of wisdom appropriate to his need.

Thus possibilities in the molecular world would be limited only by imagination, obscuring the real nature of things by the personal scenery of the mind, and by the rigidity of the sense of 'self'. For it is this latter which would prevent a man from entering into the infinite forms now open to him, just as in life a conventional bourgeois might be prevented from entering a dockside tavern or a palace reception simply by the feeling that he was 'not that sort of person'. Even in the physical world innumerable possibilities are open to man which remain unrealized, not from any actual impediment, but solely from self-doubt, worry, fear of the opinion of others and so on. Certainly such imaginary obstacles are here supported and justified by real poverty, real ill-health, real pain, and real deficiencies of body and mind. But there, in a non-physical world, there would be no such objective impediments. *All* would depend on what a man believed of himself, demanded of himself.

The man who thought of himself as a physical body would live in a shadowy simulacrum of a physical world, tortured by the impossibility of indulging what no longer existed. The man who thought of himself as a millionaire would continue to accumulate imaginary wealth and wield imaginary power, all the while burdened with the cares of preserving what he no longer possessed. On the other hand, the man who thought of himself as a mathematician would live in a world of mathematical laws, and the biologist in a world of natural ones—so that their later discoveries in the physical world might perhaps be seen as dim memories of such laws directly perceived in the super-physical worlds between death and birth.

So also the man who with his whole being believed all to exist in God, and who could completely forget his personal existence in such conviction, *might actually experience this truth*. And if he did so, it is impossible to believe that the knowledge and certainty of such an experience would ever again abandon him, no matter what the circumstances of his later birth.

VI

TIME IN THE INVISIBLE WORLDS

ALTHOUGH everything we have deduced about the invisible worlds seems both amazing and reasonable still we seem not to have broken sufficiently with our ordinary perceptions of physical life. For it must be that everything there is absolutely the *opposite*, the *reverse* and *contrary* of all we know here. It is for this very reason that that world is invisible to us, as the head of a penny *must* be invisible to one looking at its reverse, the tail.

Now the most difficult thing of all for us to conceive from an opposite point of view is time. Our usual idea of time is that there is one time flowing in one direction at one rate. We have already tried to break with the idea of one rate of flow, and have shown that there is every reason to believe that the rate of flow becomes slower and slower behind us or towards the past and faster and faster ahead or towards the future. And we have tried to see the consequences of such a speeding-up of time, and the nature of the other worlds into which this acceleration must lead.

But there remains another preconceived idea to be broken, namely that time must always flow in the same direction. In fact, once we accepted the idea that death and birth are one, that man goes back to the beginning, and embarks on a recurrence of his former life, we accepted the idea that somewhere, somehow, time can go backwards, can have a reverse flow which bears men back from their end to their origin. And this arrangement seemed implied in the mechanism of the solar system revealed by the vision of Er, who perceived whorls or spirals of planetary time moving in opposite directions, the Fate of the present spinning them one way, the Fate of the future the reverse way, and the Fate of the past now one way and now the other. In other words, one set of spirals seems to carry men *forward* through their earthly career, and the other to carry them invisibly *back* to where they started.

A second Platonic myth, however, develops the idea in much greater detail. This myth from the *Politicus* we already quoted, recalling the words of the Stranger that

this cosmos, for a certain space of time, God himself doth help to guide and propel in the circular motion thereof; and then, when the cycles of time appointed unto it have accomplished their measure, he letteth it go. Then doth it begin to go round in the contrary direction, of itself, being a living creature which hath gotten understanding from him who fashioned it in the beginning.*

This description seemed to fit with uncanny accuracy the figure of the two connecting circles, or figure of infinity, which we had evolved to symbolize the connection between the visible and invisible lives of man. But we did not examine the implications of the connection.

What does it mean that the 'circular motion' of time is reversed in the invisible world? Have we any clues to the understanding of this problem? Perhaps we have. We recall for instance, the theory developed by Ouspensky from observation of the fact that complicated dream-plots are produced by the event which wakes us up, that many if not all dreams must be dreamed *backwards*, from the end towards the beginning.† And we remember the other idea that the almost instantaneous re-experiencing of life by drowning people is also in reverse, that is, from the moment of drowning backwards towards birth.

Both of these examples evoke the principle of the cinema film and projector. A film of half an hour's duration contains as many frames or pictures as a man's life contains days, so that the analogy is a vivid one. At rest this film is wound upon a reel. Upon being passed through a projector at the proper speed, it gives the illusion of a

* *The Myths of Plato*, trs. by J. A. Stewart, p. 179
† P. D. Ouspensky: *A New Model of the Universe*, p. 289

moving image or living story, and is all the while being wound from the first reel on to a second. When the display is finished the film is now found to be wound on the second reel, *but in reverse*. In order to make ready for a second showing it must be wound back on to the first reel again. This is usually done mechanically, *at great speed*, and without using the projecting light, that is, *invisibly*, *in an invisible world*. There could be no more exact model of man's life in the two worlds. Time, in the invisible world, *must run backwards*. How can it be otherwise?

Now Plato, in the *Politicus* myth, seemed to develop the idea of time running alternately backwards and forwards as referring to different ages of the larger cosmos of the earth. But at the same time he indicated that this principle must refer to all cosmoses, including the microcosm of man. For this was the way God arranged his creation—first, the winding of a spring by a higher agency, then the running of the clock-work by mechanical laws.

In fact, taking the principle on a larger scale, Plato shows many interesting and unsuspected results of such a change. He describes very vividly the idea that it would make men earth-born, that is, men would *begin* by their elements assembling into human form underground, this form in due course being thrown up out of the grave, and in a day or so taking breath from its exposure to the air. He describes how the old would become younger, pass into maturity, youth, childhood, grow smaller and smaller and so disappear.

Plato himself does not bother to show how such reversal of time would also completely exchange the roles of different realms of nature—how plants, instead of being born from the earth and eaten by man, would then, like human beings now, appear to be *born* from men and *buried* in the earth: and how men, instead of being born of their mothers and buried in earth would, like plants, be born of earth and eaten by their mothers.

Plato simply leaves us with the principle. But the very *existence* of this principle revolutionizes our whole conception of time, cause and effect, good and evil, salvation, and every other problem which man faces. For it is an idea of such power, intensity and far-reaching effect that it could not be invented. It is too strong for human imagination, which of itself can only produce weak ideas, enervating thoughts.

Let us examine the implications of time running backward in more detail, with the idea that this must be the nature of time in the invisible world. In the first place we must examine what happens to our idea of cause and effect. Cause and effect is simply a description of different stages in a temporal sequence; what goes *before* is taken as cause, what follows *after* is taken as effect. But if time were reversed then effect would become cause, and cause effect.

Take a simple example. A man is enraged with me, he makes a bitter remark, which I hear and become offended. Reverse time. Thoughts of resentment are passing in my head; they are communicated by nervous impulse to my ear-drums, which are set vibrating, and transmit sound-waves through the air to his larynx; this vibrates in sympathy, and in turn transmits nervous impulses to his brain and solar plexus, where they are converted into thoughts and sensations of passionate anger. Lo and behold, my resentment is the *cause* of his anger. I am myself responsible for anything said to me. In me lies the cause of everything I see, hear and perceive. *I create the kind of world in which I live.*

In such a motion of time the philanthropist *takes* money from the poor and makes them destitute; the murderer *gives birth* to the murdered man, and *is responsible for the latter's life.*

What of a great author, a Shakespeare? All over the world men are filled with noble, strange and tragic thoughts and feelings. They pick up worn and dog-eared volumes, into which they transfer their higher emotions. If thousands or millions of men do this, the volumes are made new by these emotions, they come together, pass backwards through the press, decrease into smaller and smaller editions, and after centuries are compressed into a single manuscript.

This manuscript is at last found by a Shakespeare. He sets it on a table before him, turns over the pages, the words run back into his pen, whose motion produces in him an extraordinary fervour of power and understanding. When all has run back, he is filled with ecstasy and knowledge. All that millions of men have felt has entered into him: *the readers have created Shakespeare.*

What does it all mean? It means that the universe is all one, and that every part depends upon every other part, every phenomenon is connected with all other phenomena, nothing can be changed without the whole changing. It is this knowledge which gives rise to the feeling in the great saviours of humanity, the highest men, that they are *responsible* for all the evil and suffering in the world. Seen in one direction of time such men take into themselves or assimilate enormous quantities of human pain and ignorance; seen in the other direction they seem to give rise to it. This other direction they alone perceive. In that perception which belongs to the invisible world, they know that they and this vast sea of suffering are inseparable. They know that they are responsible for all that *was* before them. They know that no permanent satisfaction can be achieved by them as individuals, until the whole level of humanity is raised, until all mankind is regenerated in the *past* as well as in the future.

How is this possible? It means that the sufferers must *look forward* to their saviour, the ignorant must *anticipate* their enlightenment; they must already be healed by what *will* happen. This is the inner meaning of faith. Faith is that by which mankind relieves the intolerable burden of teachers and saviours in reversed time; that by which the level of the whole is raised.

Only with the idea of reversed time can we see the true significance of the vow of the Bodhisattva, not to enter into Nirvana until all sentient beings shall be saved, and all creatures everywhere be set upon the path of Buddhahood.*

* W. Y. Evans-Wentz: *Tibet's Great Yogi Milarepa*, p. 9

For this vow must arise from sight of the universe as it is, that is, in reversed time and above time. Only confined to our ordinary illusion of a one-way flowing time could men believe in a personal salvation and paradise independent of others and of the past.

There is another strange effect of reversed time. We already saw how sound would pass from the hearer to the speaker. But we did not then note that light would now proceed *out* of all creatures, instead of being received by them. From men, animals, plants and stones energy would arise to create light, which would now *ascend* from the earth to the sun. Everywhere heat would rise out of the rocks, colour out of flowers, ultra-violet rays from all growing things, and fusing together, would reconstitute solar radiation. Just as all life as we now know it derives from the sun, so in that other time, all life would return thither. This would be the inbreathing of Brahma of Hindu cosmology.

All this seems to correspond exactly with time after death. For there, instead of light creating essence and essence physical form, as happens in the world we now know, we deduce that physical form must be dissolved into molecular, and molecular into electronic matter. From another point of view this would mean the re-transformation of cellular bodies into sunlight, or the yielding up again of the sunlight from which they had originally been created. Just as our life evidently springs from the sun, so in the reversal of time would it inevitably return thither.

Such reversal of time, with all the effects which we have described, would seem to belong to the nature of the second or invisible circle, along which man's soul passes through the molecular world, re-living its physical life in reverse, and feeling itself as the *cause* instead of the consequence of all it previously experienced.

If we set down the two circles again, we shall see why this reversal must be so. The plane is the plane of time; motion clockwise on this plane is forward or ordinary time; motion anti-clockwise is reversed time; motion round the figure

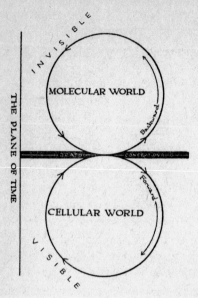

of eight or infinity must include one circle forward and one circle backward, like the winding and re-winding of the cinema film or like the whorls spun opposing ways of the vision of Er.

But is this all?

Backwards or forward it's just as far,
Within or without the path is as narrow.
Time and tide wait for no man. 'Go round about,'
Said the Boyg, and it's what I must do here.*

So cries Peer Gynt in his last extremity.

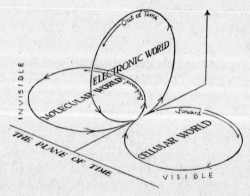

To complete our picture we must remember that there exists a third circle—the circle of the electronic world or spirit—and that this circle exists in another dimension. This other circle must rise *out of the plane of time altogether*, must lie at right angles to time. Here there will be neither forward time not backward time, because all time—past,

* Ibsen's *Peer Gynt*, trs. by Norman Ginsbury. Act V, Scene 4.

present and future—will be spread out below. Time will exist without flow, as the whole long body of the solar system, simultaneously presided over by the Fates of past, present and future, co-existed or was spread out in the sight of Er the Pamphylian.

In the third circle there can be no cause and no effect, because all is simultaneously one. Man's future is shown continuous with his past and his past with his future, as a single nerve may stretch from the brain to the fingertips and be sensed simultaneously at all points. The Bodhisattva is there inseparable from the Sudra and the Sudra from the Bodhisattva, as the heart is inseparable from the bowel and the bowel from the heart. All is there one, and only that which serves to redeem the whole can redeem a single creature.

VII

PETRIFACTION
INTO THE MINERAL WORLD

THE inconceivably terrible impression which would be created by the evil of every man's life, if intensely compressed in time, and reviewed with full realization of all the suffering resulting from it, and of *one's own fault*, has already been discussed. This sort of psychological retribution produced by a change in our perception and in our understanding of time, is in fact the only kind of hell the modern man is willing to accept. Twentieth century psychology prepares men for the idea of a subjective hell; but it does not admit the possibility of any objective hell, for which modern scientific cosmology can find no place.

Yet all the old texts which we have studied—whether Egyptian, Greek, Tibetan, Zoroastrian or Mediaeval European—are at one in supposing the existence of an actual place of retribution, a definite part of the cosmos to which those of incurably evil record are consigned after death. It is made clear in each case that this is quite a different thing from the subjective torments arising from *terror of one's own record, terror of one's own mind*, referred to above. For these are said to be felt by the soul *before judgment*, and, if understood rightly, can supposedly affect this judgment for the better. In the old terminology, this kind of suffering is 'purgatory', that is, cleansing. According to the *Tibetan Book of the Dead*, indeed, if a soul can but see this world of subjective terror and remorse for what it is, it is in that moment released from the cycle of lives and escapes judgment altogether.

The true hell, on the other hand, is always shown to be an

actual place to which the incurably evil being is consigned *after judgment*, and from which there is no return except after an immense period of suffering.

At the Egyptian judgment, for example, there awaits the monster Ammit, 'devourer of the dead', whose crocodile-jaws foreshadow all the hell-mouths of the Middle Ages. This figure, part reptile, part lion, part hippopotamus, arising from a lake of fire, is the 'eater of hearts, the devourer of the unjustified', and to the Egyptian symbolized a sort of terrible cosmic scavenger, whose function was to consume the refuse or offal of humanity. Translated to the climate and customs of Europe hell becomes represented in exactly the same sense as a *cosmic incinerator*.

These representations of hell suggest the idea that there must exist in the world of men's souls, as in every house and city, some arrangement for consuming waste matter, which would otherwise pollute and infect the whole. Some souls, we can suppose, have become too rotten or too hard to serve further in their old form, and must therefore be disposed of for the general health.

Some such disappearance out of the cycle of ordinary living and dying was visualized in our time by P. D. Ouspensky who, in discussing eternal recurrence, speaks of the possibility of a soul 'dying', 'that is, when, after many lives spent sliding down an incline, in moving along a diminishing spiral, with a quicker and quicker end, a soul ceases to be born'.*

But where would it go then? Since nothing can disappear out of the universe except with the dissolution of the whole, if a soul ceases to be born *here*, it must mean that it is born *in some other part of the cosmos*. There must be a *lower realm* than that of organic life for descending souls just as earlier, in considering molecular and electronic states of matter, we came to the conclusion that there must be *higher realms* for ascending ones.

A very vivid image of the same idea is conveyed in Zoro-

* P. D. Ouspensky: *A New Model of the Universe*, p. 497

E

astrian teaching. Here the great meeting of the ways and moment of judgment between lives is pictured as the terrible Bridge of Chinvat. Across this the righteous soul passes safely with the help of conscience. But the incurably evil soul, becoming terrified at the razor-edge, falls headlong from the middle of the bridge into the abyss of hell below. That is, it falls *out of* the circles of possible evolution.*

This image of the Bridge of Chinvat is strikingly reminiscent of the place in our diagram where the three circles of different existences join. Evidently it is possible to *fall off* at this meeting-place—to fall *down*, that is, into yet another circle in the only dimension remaining.† This circle, the opposite of the electronic or solar one, must descend into the lowest, densest, slowest and most unchangeable part of the cosmos.

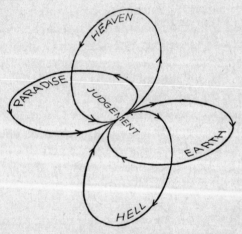

At this point we again recall the vision of Er.

They came to a certain ghostly place wherein were two open Mouths of the Earth, hard by each other, and also above, two Mouths of the Heaven, over against them: and Judges were seated between these, who, when they had given their judgments, bade the righteous take the

* The Iranian Bundahishn, quoted by J. D. C. Pavry, *The Zoroastrian Doctrine of a Future Life*, p. 93
† The Tibetan word for the hell-world, 'hung', means 'fallen'

road which leadeth to the right hand and up through Heaven . . . but the unjust they sent by the road which leadeth to the left hand and down. . . . He beheld the souls departing, some by one of the Mouths of Heaven, and some by one of the Mouths of Earth, when judgment had been given unto them; also . . . he beheld souls returning by the other two Mouths, some coming up from the Earth travel-stained, covered with dust, and some coming down from Heaven, pure.

The diagram we have evolved now emerges as an *exact representation* of what is described by Er. If we picture the circles as paths, then standing at the point of intersection—the meeting-place of all the worlds—there would indeed appear two entrances to the electronic or divine circle, one up which souls were ascending, and one from which they were returning: and equally two entrances to the unknown abysmal circle, one down which souls disappeared, and one from which they might emerge again.

Let us continue with the vision.

And he said that they all, as they came . . . turned aside with joy into the Meadow and encamped there as in a congregation. . . . So they discoursed with one another—some of them groaning and weeping when they called to mind all the terrible things they had suffered and seen in their journey under the Earth—he said their journey was for a thousand years. . . . [For] according to the number of wrongs which each man hath ever done, and the number of them he hath wronged, he payeth penalty for all in their course, ten times for each: now it is every hundred years that he payeth, for a hundred years are counted for the lifetime of a man: so it is brought to pass that the price of evil-doing is paid tenfold.*

Here exactly is the clue for which we were waiting. In hell everything is *ten times longer, ten times slower*. The world of hell is a continuation of the logarithmic progression of time that has shown us so much, *but in the opposite direction*.

So that, by analogy with divisions of the other circles, the periods marking existence in the hell-world will be roughly 80 years, 800 years, 8000 years and 80,000 years. Er, counting the possible redemption of evil lives in ten times their duration on earth, seems to visualize an escape at the

* *The Myths of Plato*, trs. by J. A. Stewart, p. 137

first break, and that souls could *die* out of the hell-world and return back to higher worlds after 800 or 1000 years, just as infants can die out of the cellular world at birth, without entering the full span of earthly life at all.

But he goes on to reveal the existence of more terrible possibilities. 'As for those who dishonoured Gods and Parents, and those who honoured them, and as for those that were murderers, he spake of their wages as being even greater.' And he gives the example of a King Ardiaeus of Pamphylia, who had killed father, brother and many others a thousand years before this time, and who now essayed to return to the upper world, but was turned back to a yet longer term and more terrible tortures. Here, even *slower time, greater duration, more extreme density* are visualized.

In the same way, the *Tibetan Book of the Dead* speaks of the immense term of existence in the hell-worlds—'falling therein, thou wilt have to endure unbearable misery, whence there is no certain time of getting out'.*

Can we imagine the significance of such *slowness* of time, as we tried to imagine the effect of the great speed of time in the molecular and electronic worlds? Decelerating time even beyond its pace in old age, we again find phenomena passing out of the compass of the organic world, whose cellular matter is not sufficiently durable for such spans of existence. The few animals which surpass two hundred years, such as the elephant and giant tortoise, have already sacrificed all finer sensibilities to sheer weight and toughness of hide and shell. Much of their anatomy is already akin to wood, which alone among cellular matter exists still longer. Certain trees—oaks and sequoias—may even endure two thousand years or more. But to do so they forgo not only the power of sensation, but also that of movement. And they are exceptions.

In a general way, we may say that the only matter to endure more than two or three centuries is of *mineral* nature. Certainly when we come to the second and third points of

* W. Y. Evans-Wentz: *The Tibetan Book of the Dead*, p. 109

this lowest circle, marked by such periods as 8000 and 80,000 years, we can think only of rocks, metals, and the *fossils* or petrified remains of once-living creatures.

This latter idea is striking. For when we recall the descriptions in all ages of the tortures of hell, the intense heat and cold, fire and ice, racking and pulverizing, and of the *indestructible* nature of the beings who must endure this for countless ages, we cannot but think that these are imaginative embroiderings on the simple idea of human souls which have in some way become *petrified*, *fossilized*, hardened beyond any hardness proper to humanity. For this implies also loss of the power to change or improve, loss of the power to respond, which we recognize as the characteristic of the greatest criminals.

Such degree of fixity or hardness has always been pictured as mineral, in such popular phrases as 'stony-hearted', 'flint-hearted', 'iron-willed', and so on. And descriptions of hell abound with such mineral and metallic metaphors, just as those of paradise do in images of air, atmosphere, breath and wind. In one Tibetan picture of hell we find sinners bowed under the weight of heavy rocks, shut in a 'doorless iron house', being filled with molten metal, dragged over iron spikes, sawn into pieces, melted down in iron cauldrons, and so on.* All these so-called 'punishments' can be paralleled in mediaeval European visions of hell, particularly in Dante's Inferno. The one thing in common about all of them is that the sufferers are always represented as in some way having been *made mineral*, or inescapably *attached to mineral forms*. And that in the process they have become as *resistant* as minerals. They have become crystallized, so that they endure endless tortures, and yet are *unable to react*, as living creatures would. As is always emphasized in ideas of hell, they cannot die. Exactly the same might be said of a piece of rock or a bar of iron.

All the 'punishments' described in fact correspond to processes by which the rigidity of minerals and metals is

* W. Y. Evans-Wentz: *The Tibetan Book of the Dead*, p. xxii

broken down in nature, and by which they are slowly cor-
roded and pulverized to the point where, as mineral salts,
they can be once again absorbed into the structure of organic life. The 'tortures of hell' might well be the description by an imaginative geologist of the transition by which,
over many thousands of years, hard granite can become fertile
loam. The melting by volcanic heat, the cracking and
splitting by intense frost, the action of icy winds, lakes of
fire, and so on—these are all geological phenomena. But
they are geological phemomena described as though human
consciousness were attached to them.

If we could make a bold leap of the imagination, we would
say that they seem to refer to human souls which, hardened
out of all semblance of humanity and robbed of all organic
sensibility by persistent crime, have in some way been *made
mineral*, entered the mineral world, and assumed a mineral
fate. So that the 'eternal' tortures now appear, not as pointless 'punishment' or 'retribution', but as a breaking down of
this wrong crystallization by the normal refining processes
of nature. The 'tortures' are due to the complete resistance
of rocks and metals to any influence less violent than that of
searing acids, of ponderous crushing and hammering, or
of terrible extremes of temperature. While 'everlasting
damnation' is a picturesque figure for the idea that *geologic*
processes and *geologic* time are here in question.

It now becomes clearer why all descriptions of hell universally place its site in the *underworld, inside the earth*. For as
we saw elsewhere, the subterranean layers of the earth represent the realm of minerals (the lithosphere) and the realm
of metals (the barysphere), enveloping an unknown core of
inconceivable density and inertia.* The descent towards
the centre of the earth is, we know scientifically, a descent
into ever increasing density. This is indeed the principle
expressed by Dante in his description of Inferno, which,
situated in the interior of the earth, he pictured as consisting
of concentric spheres of ever increasing density leading

* *The Theory of Celestial Influence*, Ch. 10

> Towards the middle, at whose point unites
> All heavy substance. . . .
> That point, to which from every part is dragged
> All heavy substance.*

This is, of course, the centre of the earth's core, which Dante, personifying the whole idea of density and gravity, makes the home of Satan, the ultimate evil.

This core of the earth is not only the region of greatest density in our world, but also that furthest removed from the light of the sun, the source of all life. It is the realm of 'Stygian darkness', one of the chief horrors of which is simply *absence of light*. 'The light of the world I shall no more see', as is said in the 'Orologium Sapientiae', 'passing all torments and pains, it grieveth me most the absence of the blessed Face of God'.†

The only place in our world where sunlight *never* penetrates is indeed the interior of the earth, and anyone who has descended into mines or deep caverns will already understand emotionally what this implies. Even so little below the earth's surface, what becomes almost unbearable after a while, is not only the complete absence of familiar form and colour, of nature and growth, which are dependent on light, but also the strange sense that *happiness is impossible there*. Light is evidently in some way *food* for the emotional side of man, and we can only take the idea of his consignment to a lightless hell to symbolize the fact that this side of him has *already died*.

All descriptions of hell combine these three ideas in one way or another—the idea of a subterranean mineral or volcanic realm, the idea of darkness, and the idea that time there is immensely long, everlasting, endless, in comparison with human measurements of time. This is the Hindu Naraka 'situated beneath the earth and beneath the waters'.‡ This is the Babylonian Aralu, 'the land of No-return, the region of

---

* Dante Alighieri: 'Inferno', Canto xxxii, line 72 and Canto xxxiv, line 105
† 'Orologium Sapientiae', in *The Book of the Craft of Dying*, ed. F. M. M. Comper, p. 119.   ‡ 'The Vishnu Purana', trs. by H. H. Wilson, Book II, Ch. V, 2. p. 214

darkness . . . the house whose enterer goes not forth . . . the road whence the wayfarer never returns . . . the house whose inhabitants see no light . . . the region where dust is their bread and their food mud'.* This is the Greek Tartarus to which the Mouth of Earth led, 'where much fire floweth, and there are great rivers of fire, and many rivers of running mud . . . a cavern in the earth, which is the greatest of them all, and, moreover, pierceth right through the Earth . . . Whoso are deemed incurable the appointed Angel doth cast into Tartarus, and thence they come not out at all'.† This is the Egyptian Amentet, represented in the cosmological plan of the Great Pyramid by a dark rocky chamber a hundred feet below ground level, whose floor is left formless and from which a final passage leads *to nothing at all*.‡

From here there is no possible way *further*. This is the end, the place where petrified souls are 'melted down' by the cosmic process which Ibsen symbolized as the Button-Moulder in *Peer Gynt*. Such 'melting down' of rigid forms, of that which has lost its power to develop, must inevitably involve tremendous suffering. Hell, as far as we can judge, is a picturization from the human point of view, of this cosmic 'melting-pot'. The purpose of hell, then, would be to restore faulty psychic products to their original state of sound raw material, which in due course could be used again, that is, re-absorbed into growing forms.

We already spoke of the process by which granite may become loam, and this in turn be incorporated into plants and animals. Such an idea is given exactly this psychic connotation in the *Vishnu Purana*:

The various stages of existence . . . are inanimate things, fish, birds, animals, men, holy men, gods, and liberated spirits; each in succession a thousand times superior to that which precedes it: and through these stages the beings that are . . . in hell are destined to proceed, until final emancipation is obtained.§

* Ishtar's Descent to Aralu, quoted by Lewis Spence, *Myths of Babylon and Assyria*, p. 130.
† *The Myths of Plato*, trs. by J. A. Stewart, pp. 87-91
‡ I. E. S. Edwards: *The Pyramids of Egypt*, p. 88
§ *The Vishnu Purana*, trs. by H. H. Wilson, Book II, Ch. VI, Vol. 5, p. 221

The descent into hell is thus a journey backwards through evolution; a sinking into ever greater density, darkness, rigidity, and inconceivable tedium of time; a falling back through the ages into primeval chaos, whence the immense ascent towards the knowledge of God has to be begun all over again from the beginning.

VIII

THE JUDGMENT OR RE-EMBODIMENT

IN all teachings the idea of Judgment introduces the conception of a *final settlement* for each life. Passage through the worlds of the spirit and of the soul, may give the individual self quite new opportunities to perceive the cosmos as it is, to judge its own nature in relation to this reality, and to revise its attitude or in religious language 'repent' accordingly. How much the self can derive from these super-physical lives must depend upon its preparation and its degree of freedom from a purely material viewpoint. All this will be subjective, and during this time the fate of the individual is, as it were, in a state of suspense.

Then, as the circles turn once more towards the inception of physical life, ever nearer comes the moment when all must congeal, crystallize, take static form. We may compare the spirit in the electronic world to the state of steam, and the soul in the molecular world to the state of water. All the while temperature is falling, processes are growing slower and slower. Suddenly, at a moment exactly known to physics, freezing takes place—that is, the liquid is endowed with *form*. This form depends upon the situation in which the water finds itself at the moment of freezing, whether in a bowl, a pipe, or in free drops on the window-pane. But once frozen, once 'embodied', nothing can then be changed but by re-heating to a higher temperature—that is, until the ice *dies* once more. The moment of freezing may be regarded as 'judgment' for the water.

For the individual self such a judgment will be its crystallization into a certain kind of physical body. For once so endowed, its manner of perception, its possibilities, probably its whole fate, will be determined by the 'type' of this body—whether ponderous, impulsive, full-blooded, sensitive, defective or whatever. Now modern embryology, striving to discover the point at which such fundamental characteristics become incipient, is forced back to the very moment of conception. For it is already here, we are told, that the chromosomes, together with their hundreds of feature-forming genes, fly together into an individual and immutable pattern.

At no later point can individuality be said to enter. For the seeds of it have already been sown, and thereafter can develop in no other way than they do develop. Our detailed study of growth only served to reveal an *unfolding* process, like that demonstrated by Japanese paper flowers when dropped in water.* The signature of the whole later body was already written in the convulsive motion of conception. So that it is this moment, if any, which must be seen as the judgment or freezing of the characteristics of individual being into permanent form.

In the *Tibetan Book of the Dead*, immediately before the picturing of the Judgment-scene, there is a very vivid description of the longing of a disembodied soul for a body:

> Thou wilt . . . think, 'Now I am dead! What shall I do?' and being oppressed with intense sorrow . . . thou wilt be wandering about hither and thither seeking a body.†

It is this very yearning, according to the Tibetan teaching, which precipitates the crystallization to which we have referred.

There follows a description of Judgment itself, from which at once 'one will wander to the doors of wombs. . . . O nobly born, at this time thou wilt see visions of males and females in union . . . In whatever continent or place thou art to be born, the signs of that birthplace will shine upon thee then.' Coincident with Judgment the self is thus represented as being irresistibly sucked into the womb from

---

* *The Theory of Celestial Influence*, Ch. 12
† W. Y. Evans-Wentz: *The Tibetan Book of the Dead*, pp. 165, 175-7

which it is destined to be born, just as in the Myth of Er the souls startled by thunder and earthquake, 'of a sudden flew up thence into divers parts to be born in the flesh, shooting like meteors'.*

This idea of Judgment as being the moment of the soul's assignment to a definite body is echoed in the particular appeal made at the Egyptian ritual to the god Khnemu, creator of bodies, who in one place is shown in the very act of fashioning man upon a potter's wheel.†

But is this re-creation of an organic body the only possible outcome of Judgment? What other sentences could be there imposed? If we return to our diagram of the four circles of heaven, purgatory, earth and hell, with their respective time-scales; and we picture Judgment as taking place at the meeting-point of these worlds, we seem to see three directions in which the self can proceed or become embodied. Having completed its cycle of lives in successive states of matter and being now about to enter upon a new cycle, it would appear to have three choices of rebirth—by ascent into the heaven-world, by descent into the hell-world, or by re-entrance into the earth-world in a body similar to that which it tenanted before.

These three roads from the fateful Chinvat Bridge are expressed with almost naïve clarity in Zoroastrian legend:

> Everyone whose good works are three grams more than his sin, goes to Heaven; everyone whose sin is more goes to Hell; whereas he in whom both are equal, remains in the Hamistikan till the future body or resurrection.‡

If we accept the idea of these three possibilities or roads we can understand why it is that the various conceptions of the fate of the soul after death which have ruled in different ages *appear* so contradictory. For different peoples and different religions, by their type and nature, have nearly al-

---

* *The Myths of Plato*, trs. by J. A. Stewart, p. 151

† Sir E. A. Wallis Budge: *Egyptian Ideas of the Future Life*, p. 118

‡ Artāk Virāz Namāk, quoted by J. D. C. Pavry, *The Zoroastrian Doctrine of a Future Life*, p. 91

ways magnified one or other or two of these possibilities, and almost never succeeded in considering all three equally.

Thus for thousands of years Egyptian nobles had expressed upon their mummies the conviction that they had abstained from all evil, would be vindicated at the Judgment, and must certainly *become Osiris*, that is, enter the heaven-world. Deification or heaven came to be represented as the normal goal of the soul of a man of a certain caste, and the other once-equal possibilities faded into forgetfulness. In late mediaeval Christianity, on the other hand, the doctrine of hell became so luridly exaggerated that only a life of special saintliness was supposed to save man from the terrible *descensus in Averno*.

Yet again, in our own time, those philosophers who have studied these matters with any degree of authenticity, like Nietzsche and particularly Ouspensky, stress the idea of recurrence or re-entry into a similar circle of physical life as the norm, and omit the idea of heaven and hell almost entirely. In view of the mediocrity of the great mass of ordinary lives, this last view may indeed be more generally applicable.

On the other hand it is only in the acceptance of three possible fates of the self, with all the cosmic pattern upon which these possibilities depend, that all the above views can be united and reconciled.

We can now understand why all the truly traditional representations of Judgment seem so extraordinarily complicated. It is because they strive to symbolize in a single whole the three fates—liberation, damnation, and human rebirth or recurrence—which lie open to the disembodied soul. In order to show this, those who originated these extraordinary compositions had to picture also the different parts of the universe with which these different fates are connected, and their relation to each other; as we have attempted to do in very simplified form by the four conjoined circles of different time.

Thus from one point of view these images of Judgment

were designed to symbolize a final allocation of the being of man after each round of existence. While secondly they tried to display the whole hierarchy of worlds—from mineral to electronic, from hell to heaven—to one of which the record, the yearnings, and the fundamental affinity of the self inevitably consign it.

Judgment was then portrayed as the solemn moment when all a man's constituent parts, and all his past record of good, evil and indifference, are brought together and sealed into an appropriate organism and form of existence. All such accounts emphasize that at this juncture, every aspect of man, even the most secret and hidden, of whose very existence he is normally unaware, must come together and bear witness concerning him.

About this subjective or self-condemning aspect of Judgment the *Tibetan Book of the Dead* is again most specific. For here a very detailed and symbolic Judgment-scene is pictured, presided over by Yama-Raja, the flaming Lord of Death, at which the good and evil deeds of the deceased are weighed against each other by monkey and bull-headed powers, in the presence of deities, furies, advocates and accusers. At the end of this account, however, the following extraordinary warning is added:

> Apart from one's own hallucinations, in reality there are no such things existing outside oneself as Lord of Death, or god, or demon, or the Bull-headed Spirit of Death. Act so as to recognize this.*

Judgment is thus a drama played by the different sides of man's own nature, and in which his own different functions or powers stand as accused, accuser, tormentor, defender, and recording angel. This idea was intentionally adapted in certain mediaeval writings, such as the *Lamentation of the Dying Creature* where the dying creature, his good angel, his conscience, his soul, and his five senses are represented as acting out a kind of *dress rehearsal* for the true Judgment which will follow after death.†

* W. Y. Evans-Wentz: *The Tibetan Book of the Dead*, p. 167
† *The Book of the Craft of Dying*, edited by F. M. M. Comper, p. 137

We are struck by the way in which descriptions separated by thousands of years and originating in widely separated continents tally in their enumeration of the different parts of man. And we are still further astonished by the complexity of man's structure as there represented.

In every case Judgment is shown as taking place under the presidence of a superhuman being, who is as it were the lord, protector and saviour of mankind. In the Christian Judgment this figure is Christ, in the Egyptian Osiris, in the Greek Zeus, in the Zoroastrian Ahura Mazda, and in the Tibetan Yama-Raja.* In each case this presiding being is both god made man and man made god, the archetype of divinity incarnate and the example of man who has become divine. He represents at the same time divinity for mankind, and the potential divinity of the actual soul now come to Judgment. He is both universal spirit, and the spirit by which this individual can become one with that universe in the electronic world.

Before this divine president there takes place that process which is universally pictured as a *weighing in the balance*. Weighing represents a judgment which is absolutely impersonal, an objective measure of density. It is the assessment of man's being by the operation of natural laws. These laws, by which the lighter and warmer inevitably rises, and the denser and colder inexorably falls, are personified in the Judgment-scene by the operator of the scales—the Christian St. Michael, the Zoroastrian Rashnu, Anubis the wolf-headed in Egypt, and Shinje the monkey-headed in Tibet.

Sometimes a triad of guardians of the scales conveys still more vividly the impression of a natural process, produced by the interaction of three forces. In the Tibetan weighing, Shinje is associated with Wang-gochan the bull-headed and Dul-gochan the serpent-headed; in the Zoroastrian, the angels Mithra and Sraosha aid 'Rashnu the just, who held in

* Yama-Raja in his earthly or manly aspect is Chenrezigs who is said to incarnate in the Dalai Lamas; as Christ in his manly aspect lived in Palestine at the beginning of our era.

his hand the yellow golden balance, and weighed the righteous and the wicked'.* While in the Greek, Rhadamanthus,
Aeacus and Minos sit together in the Meadow at the Part-
ing of the Ways, the first to judge the Asiatic dead, the
second the dead of the white race, and the third 'in the
chief place' to act as final arbiter.†

But what is this which is so inexorably weighed? In the
Zoroastrian version it is the evil works, words and thoughts
of the dead man which are thus weighed against the good.
In the Tibetan scene an evil genius empties a sack of black
pebbles, the evil deeds of the deceased, into one scale, while
the good genius or guardian angel empties a sack of white
pebbles, his good deeds, into the other.

Such ideas are familiar. But they become extremely interesting when in the latter case such adjudgment of deeds is
combined with the idea of the *Mirror of Karma*, in which the
judges may see the whole of the man's earthly life displayed
and against which photographic record there is no possible
appeal. For this mirror or film of the past life is held by
the Lord of Death, Yama-Raja,‡ who, as we said earlier,
represents divinity or spirit, the electronic state in which a
whole life can be lived in forty minutes. The Mirror of
Karma, like the tablet borne by the souls in the Myth of Er§
and like the palette of Thoth, the Egyptian scribe of the
gods,¶ is a direct reference to this recording of life in an intensely compressed form. So also El Greco, in his 'Martyrdom of St. Maurice', could show above the great funnel of
light by which the soul of the martyr will ascend to heaven,
a recording angel singing the *libretto* or *chord* of his completed life.** Such compressed record ensures that connections and consequences are inescapably seen, and that judg-

---

* Artāk Virāz Namāk, quoted by J. D. C. Pavry, *The Zoroastrian Doctrine of a
Future Life*, p. 85
† *The Myths of Plato*, trs. by J. A. Stewart, p. 119 and p. 135
‡ W. Y. Evans-Wentz: *The Tibetan Book of the Dead*, p. xxi
§ *The Myths of Plato*, trs. by J. A. Stewart, p. 135
¶ Sir E. A. Wallis Budge: *The Egyptian Book of the Dead*, pp. 25-6
** El Greco: 'The Martyrdom of St. Maurice', in the Escorial, 1580-4

ment is absolute, because no evidence is lacking and no act forgotten.

But the Egyptian picture of judgment, which is probably the oldest, represents an even more subtle complex of ideas. For here it is the *heart* of the dead man which is weighed, and since his soul and the form of his old body are shown separately, as looking on, this heart seems to indicate something independent of either, that is, something akin to the very *inner quality* of the man, his being.* This heart is weighed against the feather of Maat, which seems similar in sense to the Buddhist dharma, that is, right, truth, and particularly, what the individual *should be*, his right-way or true potentiality. The being that the man has evolved for himself is thus measured against his original capacity, just as it is in the parable of the talents.†

Looking on at this fateful balancing are shown the other parts of the dead man. His 'luck' or physical destiny stands below; his spirit, a man-headed hawk, flies above. While between these, watched over by Renenet and Meskhenet, the goddesses of birth, lies a small unshapen block with a human face, *the embryo of his next body waiting to receive the impress which the judgment shall determine.*

In this extraordinary figure is not only shown the weighing of a man's acquired being against his original capacity, but also how the excess or deficiency so manifest exactly determines the new body into which the self will next be born, that is, *its orginal capacity in the coming life.* So is the circle complete, and the result or reward of this judgment is already that which will enter the right-hand scale at the next. Judgment is recurrent, justice eternal, and a new weighing springs out of the old, world without end.

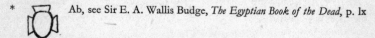

*   Ab, see Sir E. A. Wallis Budge, *The Egyptian Book of the Dead*, p. lx

† St. Luke, xix.11

F

IX

RECURRENCE
INTO THE ORGANIC WORLD

SO far we have thought of judgment or the allotment of new forms in a philosophical way. But when we approach the problem from the other side, and see men born and apparently conceived with an innate capacity for music like Mozart, for mathematical thought like Newton, for exploration like Columbus, or on the other hand with physical deficiencies of organ or limb, or with untraceable predispositions to vice or cruelty, we are forced to consider the problem from a practical point of view. Somewhere, in another world, the fundamental chord of a man's life has sounded, and here in this world the physical constituents of his organism have assumed the responding pattern and become tangible to us.

At the moment of death, says one Tibetan doctrine,

the four sounds called 'awe-inspiring sounds' are heard: from the vital-force of the earth-element, a sound like the crumbling down of a mountain; from the vital-force of the water-element, a sound like the breaking of ocean waves; from the vital-force of the fire-element, a sound as of a jungle afire; from the vital-force of the air-element, a sound like a thousand thunders reverberating simultaneously.

The place that one getteth into in fleeing from these sounds, is the womb.*

The same transmission of man's essence backwards to conception by the intense energy generated at death is described in Sankya:

The latencies (or unfulfilled effects) of karma done during the life that is drawing to a close form the karmasya (Physical potential) of the

*W. Y. Evans-Wentz:' The Yoga of the After-Death State', in *Tibetan Yoga and Secret Doctrine*, p. 242

74

next. But it takes shape by intrinsic rearrangement at the time the linga (essence) leaves the body.   The stimuli generated by the detachment of the linga, which has been described as being felt like the breaking of innumerable cords, at the moment of death, cause the reappearance or recollection of all latencies of the life that is just over.   The linga is then freed from the physical body . . . and all the latencies appear in a moment rearranged according to their character and strength, the consistency of the mind at that moment being likened to that of electric fluid.   This happens by a single impulse in a single moment and therefore the whole and its parts are cognized in one and the same moment.   Thus connected, the latencies form the karmasya, or the physical energy for the construction of the next body.*

In some way the disintegration of the earthly elements of the old body appears to set up a vibration which can pass invisibly *through time*, just as radio-waves can pass invisibly through space. This vibration would seem to be the bearer of the final psychological pattern of the dying man, as the carrier-wave of a television-transmitting-station bears invisibly the image of the performing artist, which, received by suitable apparatus, is endowed with visible form many hundred miles from where he actually exists. The suitable apparatus for the reception of the psychic pattern transmitted by the individual at death, is the very ovum from which he is to spring, raised to an extraordinary pitch of sensitivity by the sexual act of the parents.

How does the reception of this pattern of individuality appear to science? In the first moment of fertilization the tiny dart of the spermatozoon is seen to plunge through the skin of the ovum which instantly closes over it once more. There it sets up a field of attraction, drawing and drawn inexorably to the female nucleus which awaits it at the centre of the egg. As these two nuclei merge into microscopic unity, the intricate filaments or chromosomes of which they are composed perform an ecstatic dance, untangling, separating and re-pairing in the instant. Too fast for calculation all falls like lightning into a new design—the sign or symbol of the man-to-be.

* Srimad Vivekaprasada Brahmacari: *The Samkhya Catechism*, p. 90

Of these chromosomes each ordinary cell of the human body contains forty-eight, or twenty-four pairs. The reproductive cells, however, contain but a single chromosome from each pair, thus in their union yielding the *new combination* of forty-eight which makes each embryo unique and each man original.

What are these chromosomes, each of which bears the sign of some function, quality or form, and which welded in perfect harmony compose the whole? Little is proven of the sphere of influence of each. But one pair is known to determine sex, for it is the completeness of this pair which makes female, an odd one male—as in the biblical legend of Eve made from Adam's rib and having one more rib than he. So that the field of influence of the other chromosomes must presumably refer to features or qualities as fundamental as that of sex.

Remember, for example, the eight main functions and systems of man as outlined in the first chapter.* Suppose three aspects of each function—an 'automatic' or mechanical aspect, an 'artistic' or emotional aspect, and an 'inventive' or intellectual aspect—and further suppose each aspect governed by positive and negative poles. In this way we reach a total of forty-eight main 'controls', which between them might determine the development of every side of the human machine. Whether or not this division be correct, here is the scale on which a chromosome may be expected to exercise its influence.

But modern biology divides each chromosome into half-hypothetical particles called genes, which supposedly control much finer divisions of the organism. A hundred or more such genes make up a single chromosome. So that if we consider the different aspects and positive and negative sides of each anatomical system as controlled by half a dozen chromosomes, one gene would determine but a six-hundredth part of such a system. Here we appear to be reaching as fine divisions as the tilt of a nose, the timbre of vocal

* Page 8

chords, or a tendency to sea-sickness. A few thousand such details and you have the man complete. And just as the quotations of a few thousand stocks and shares can give an exact reflection of the economic life of the whole world on any given day, so the index provided by a few thousand genes—by reference to some cosmic cipher which is unknown to us—might well indicate the whole constitution of a man.

There is a further important point about the genes. They are so small as to consist of no more than a few—perhaps half a dozen—molecules. That is to say, they belong to the molecular world, and obey molecular laws. It is this which makes them so elusive of study. They lie beyond the cellular or organic world to which our observation is confined.

Remember how it was shown that returning towards the moment of conception we come to a point where processes work too fast to be contained within cellular matter, that faster than this they must escape into matter in molecular state. Genes and chromosomes represent the first entry of human life into our field of physical observation. They lie on the boundary of the two worlds, partly partaking of the nature of matter in its free molecular state, partly confined within that aboriginal cell, the fertilized ovum.

Is there any scientific evidence to support the idea that these molecular keys are controlled *across time, out of the future?* Until recently it was not known what kind of influences or radiations might be expected to affect the genes. But in late years rearrangements or alterations of the genes of tulips, for example, have been obtained by subjecting them to X-rays or radium. As a result of such treatment sports or mutations of quite new shapes, forms and colours have been artificially obtained. One of the terrors of the atomic bomb is that its rays play tricks with the very stability of the human form. In some way radiation of this particular wave-length affects the disposition of the genes and produces startling changes in what we regard as individuality.

Now one of the peculiarities of such radio-active frequencies is that, unlike radiations of sound, heat or light, they persist through long periods of time. The half period of radium, for example, is 1600 years, which means that it takes 1600 years for the radiation of a particle of radium to diminish by half. Put in another way, the vibrations set up by radium fade in a millennium about as much as the reverberation of a great bell might fade in half a minute. Just as the note of the bell passes through thirty seconds, such radio-active emanation has *passed through* 1600 *years*.

This means that the same radiation which can affect the genes of a tulip now, could also produce a similar sport a thousand years hence. Or conversely, the same radioactivity that could produce the monstrous tulip then, can create an identical change to-day. Has the formative influence travelled backwards or forwards through time? It is the same thing. One can only say that this radiation, which has power over form, is *independent of time*.

Later we shall see this as an example of the general principle that form in one world is created by influence from the world above, that molecular arrangements can only be altered by electronic force. Meanwhile, we have a perfectly scientific basis for the proposition with which we began—namely, that formative influences released by death must travel backwards and *re-make the embryo*: and that this must be done by instantaneous manipulation of the genes at the moment of conception.

How could such influences be expected to act? We may suppose that at the end of life, each psychological feature of man has become either exaggerated or diminished, as compared with the organic tendency inherent in him at birth. Either he will have struggled to overcome some deficiency or weakness, or it will have gained still more power over him. Either he will have endeavoured to restrain an overmastering tendency, or he will be more than ever at its mercy. And since every psychological feature corresponds to some actual physical feature, it means that in the intensely compressed 'code' of the organism provided by the genes, the particular gene ruling this feature will at the close of life be due either for increased or decreased stimulation.

In this way we can imagine the jaw of the prize-fighter growing with each life a fraction larger, the flesh of the glutton grosser, the ear of the musician keener, the word-memory of the author more perfect. By the ever-increasing familiarity of repetition, it could only be expected that those features which are already most developed would continue to develop further, and at death signal a still stronger impulse back to the corresponding gene awaiting in the dance of conception.

It is no doubt in this sense that the symbology of animal rebirth was used in various teachings. Each animal was taken as the extreme exaggeration of one feature, both physical and psychological. Thus the dog might symbolize the nose, the power of scent, and also the state of being utterly in the power of this function, that is, at the mercy of animal lusts which are largely stimulated by scents. In the same way a snake might symbolize the glandular combination which makes for darting and vicious reactions. Thus each animal would represent the pathological exaggeration of a feature controlled by one gene or set of genes, out of all harmony with the rest of the organism, and blindly assuming mastery of the whole.

In the Myth of Er it is described how many of the souls of Greek heroes, offered a free choice from all possible examples of lives, chose those of animals corresponding to their nature—Ajax that of a lion, Agamemnon of an eagle, and Epeius, the jester, of an ape.* As one reads, one does indeed have a terrible impression of Ajax growing ever shaggier and more stupidly brave, Agamemnon more lonely, silent and aquiline, Epeius more facile and pointless in his mimicry, from life to life for all eternity. This is the terrible idea which was conveyed by the ancients in the guise of

* The Myths of Plato, trs. by J. A. Stewart, p. 149

animal transmigration—that of ever-growing fixity in *one particular feature*.

'If one entereth into the womb through the feelings of attachment and repulsion,' says the *Tibetan Book of the Dead*, 'one may be born either as a horse, a fowl, a dog, or a human being'.* Here we have the idea of human rebirth as a failure—from the point of view of those attempting to escape into the electronic or heaven-world altogether—but in contrast to the symbolism of animal rebirth, as at least a *balanced* failure, in which all the different features of the human organism are transmitted more or less in their right relation and proportion.

This idea of increased balance of features, increased harmony of the organism, however, already implies a high degree of self-knowlege on the part of the individual, combined with intentional struggle against known weaknesses and intentional cultivation of known deficiencies.

We can now see better how the mechanism of human recurrence might work; how the 'latencies' of the past life, 'arranged according to their character and strength', as the Sankhya account has it, could be transmitted at death feature by feature to the appropriate genes and chromosomes within the egg. And we further see how the total of this message, composed of some thousands of such signs, could be carried instantaneously through time by a radiation enjoying such permanence and penetration as we now know to belong to radio-activity.

But the act of conception is also the sexual act of the parents. The creation of the new pattern or field of force derives also from them, and their state, the intensity and purity of their emotion and so on. So that, if some serious improvement and harmonizing of the new embryo in relation to the old is to be achieved, we come to the idea that the dying man must not only have begun to master his own weaknesses, but he must also in some way *raise his own parents to a higher level*. He must teach his parents now, to make his

---

* W. Y. Evans-Wentz: *The Tibetan Book of the Dead*, p. 178

next body better. And he must bring such intensity of consciousness and emotion to the moment of his own conception, *that it communicates itself to them.*

This mysterious idea is referred to in the *Tibetan Book of the Dead* thus:

... direct thy wish, and enter into the womb. At the same time, emit thy gift-waves [of grace or goodwill] upon the womb which thou art entering, [transforming it thereby] into a celestial mansion.*

Highest man cannot wait. He must improve his own heredity, *arrange his own birth.*

For men neither saints nor criminals, we see by contrast only a gradual and perhaps imperceptible change from life to life—either by one feature tending to swallow up the rest, or on the contrary, by a slow inclination towards harmony and balance of the whole. This is the eternal recurrence which Nietzsche described, and which Ouspensky evoked in his novel *Strange Life of Ivan Osokin.*

But for how many lives is it possible to expect such imperceptible changes to apply? As we know from the graphs of every vital process, nothing in nature follows a straight incline for ever; but sooner or later curves into soaring ascent or plunging fall. How patient is nature in man's case? How many lives may be expected to enjoy before a final accounting, a judgment of judgments, is required?

Even here the old legends leave us not without a clue.

Now into the same Place from which each Soul cometh, [it is written in the Phaedrus myth,] she returneth not again until ten thousand years have been accomplished; for sooner is no Soul fledged with wings, save the Soul of him who hath sought after True Wisdom without deceit, or hath loved his Comrade in the bonds of Wisdom. The Souls of such men, when the third course of a thousand years is finished, if they have chosen this life three times in order, being fledged with wings, do then depart.†

What could this mean? Ten thousand years, according to the reckoning specifically mentioned in the parallel Myth of Er, is a hundred lives. Such a calculation might pass

* W. Y. Evans-Wentz: *The Tibetan Book of the Dead,* p. 191
† *The Myths of Plato,* trs. by J. A. Stewart, p. 317

unnoticed did it not surprisingly remind us of the one hundred and eight beads on the necklace of Buddha, each bead symbolizing a reincarnation.

In any case the passage appears to suggest for the mass of mankind an immensely long period, amounting perhaps to a century of lives, in which the slow tide affecting humanity in general may be expected to have done its work or failed to do so. In improvement on this scale there is nothing personal, man being apparently offered the opportunity of participating in some general and imperceptible ascent at the tempo of processes applying to all nature.

At the same time a quicker way, or short cut, so to speak, seems to be visualized 'for those who have sought after True Wisdom without deceit'. Such men, having accomplished a third of the total lives allotted to them, seem to be introduced to a different chance. They may be presented with the opportunity of contact with a teacher or a school, and in this way learn the secret of regeneration. With special knowledge, exact guidance, intense work on themselves, and luck, they may perhaps go up by a direct way, *escape out of the cycle of rebirth*. This is the possibility pictured in the old Russian ikons of the Second Dread Coming, where a few monks, avoiding the general judgment, are shown *flying vertically up the right-hand margin direct to heaven*.*

But for those who have learned this secret time is immediately counted by a different measure. It is no longer a question of scores of lives. A special chance is revealed, but it must be utilized *very quickly*. Some definite level must be achieved in a very few lives. 'The Souls of such men . . . if they have chosen this life three times in order, being fledged with wings, do then depart.'

It is strange to find this fascinating and terrible idea exactly echoed twenty-five centuries later in our own most sceptical time. In Ouspensky's *Strange Life of Ivan Osokin*, the hero has at last come to see with tragic clarity the ever-returning circle of his own life. He meets a magician who

* N. P. Kondakov: *The Russian Icon*, plate LXIII

explains to him something more. But in his excitement at learning this, he hardly hears the latter add:

A man who has begun to guess the great secret must make use of it, otherwise it turns against him. It is not a safe secret. When one has become aware of it, one must go on or one will go down. When one finds the secret or hears about it, one has only two or three or in any case only a few more lives.

X

MEMORY
IN THE INVISIBLE WORLDS

FIRST of all, we must try to understand that 'memory' can only refer to those denser worlds, in which perception travels through time slowly enough to yield a sense of past, present and future. In the electronic world there can be no memory, because everything is *now* and everything known. From this highest point of view it is incorrect to think of the different lives of man in sequence: it is a question of *simultaneous recurrence*.

Yet in the world in which we live we cannot think in this way: we have to suppose before and after, one life succeeding another. And in such a world our nearest approximation to higher perception is exactly 'memory'.

We have already studied the problem of consciousness and memory within the span of one life—how moments of more vivid consciousness of one's existence within the surrounding world set up pulses, which as it were run after the ordinary progress of perception through time, and catch up with it in the form of 'memories'. We also supposed that such moments extraordinarily intensified—perhaps by great joy, tragedy, surprise or strangeness—might even radiate an impulse of memory to a corresponding point on the spiral of another life, thus giving rise to all the strange sensations of *familiarity* with unknown events and scenes and even to *foresight* of things about to happen in the immediate future.*

But all serious studies of the nature of memory always sooner or later come up against the blank walls of birth and

---

* Scores of such documented stories were collected by the late Camille Flammarion in his book *Death and its Mystery*, though unfortunately from a slightly morbid point of view.

death. We can build up an almost overwhelming mass of evidence to suggest that successive lives develop one out of another in recurrence, and that the moment of death in one life is the moment of conception in the next. But we can never prove it, for the reason that the memory of ordinary men can never surpass this obstacle. For familiar levels of consciousness and for the impulses of memory arising from them death is an *absolute insulator*. To pass through death into the next life memory would have to be of far greater force, that is, it would have to arise from an immensely higher intensity of consciousness than any we ordinarily know.

We may compare the circle of man's life to an electric circuit which is broken at death, and memory to the current. This 'break' is quite sufficient to prevent the flow of current at its ordinary intensity from one side to the other. But were the electric tension to be *very greatly* increased, the current might be expected to arc across the gap, thus creating an intense light and at the same time completing the circuit and permitting a 'flow' from one side to the other.

Nearly all traditions about the adventures of the soul after death contain some reference, often unnoticed, to a point where memory is *removed or washed away*. The vision of St. Makary of Alexandria, for example, describes how the soul after spending three days becoming freed from the body and after ascending to heaven for the adoration of God, is then commanded to wander for six days in paradise where, 'contemplating it all, it becomes transformed and *forgets all the sorrows it had while in the body*'.

Here we can very well trace a degenerate version of a true legend, for in this vision the natural human tendency and desire to forget unhappiness is justified, and loss of memory at a definite point is now made to seem something desirable, instead of something mortally dangerous and to be avoided. The whole meaning of the story is thus turned upside down, for the point of all original legends is exactly that at this time memory must at all costs be *retained*.

This mistake, however, gives us a very interesting idea of how loss of memory may come about. For in this vision, forgetfulness is connected with the world of 'paradise', that is, the molecular world, in which we supposed the soul to relive or review its past life in intensely compressed form. We earlier realized the terrible emotional anguish which would be connected with such intense concentration of memory in all ordinary lives, and we can understand that the compelling desire of the self at this time would be to escape from this unbearable remorse, *not to remember any more, to forget at all costs.*

In Ouspensky's symbolic novel about recurrence, the hero who passionately desires the chance to return over his wasted life, with full memory of all his mistakes, at last finds a magician who agrees to send him back as he wishes. 'And you will remember everything,' adds the magician, *'as long as you do not wish to forget.'** This absolutely fundamental principle which governs all manifestations of memory in life, must apply with a hundredfold greater force to memory beyond death.

This idea of an intense desire to forget, of a passionate longing after forgetfulness is vividly conveyed in the Greek legend of Lethe.

Thence, Er said, [the soul of] each man, without turning back, went straight on under the throne of Necessity, and when each, even unto the last, was come out through it, they altogether journeyed to the Plain of Lethe, through terrible burning heat and frost; and this Plain is without trees or any herb that the earth bringeth forth. He said that they encamped, when it was already evening, beside the River of Forgetfulness, the water whereof no pitcher holdeth. Now it was necessary that all should drink a certain measure of the water; but they that were not preserved by wisdom drank more than the measure; and as each man drank *he forgot all.*†

This, however, is an incomplete version of the more esoteric Orphic legend of *two* streams from which the dead might drink—Lethe and Mnemosyne, oblivion and memory.

* P. D. Ouspensky: *Strange Life of Ivan Osokin*, p. 20
† *The Myths of Plato*, trs. by J. A. Stewart, pp. 151 and 156

For in the famous golden tablet found at Petelia, exact in-structions are given to the Orphic initiate whose goal, having become purified, is *to escape from the cycle of incar-nations altogether*.* Such a candidate must carefully avoid the free-flowing fountain on the left hand with a white cypress growing near it, and instead address himself to the guard-ians of the hidden well of Mnemosyne in these striking words: 'I am the child of Earth and Heaven: I am parched with thirst; I perish; give me cool water to drink from the well of Memory.' And the guardians will give him water to drink from the holy well, and he will be translated to dwell for ever with the Heroes.

Exactly so does the Russian Service for the Dead con-clude: 'Give rest eternal in blessed falling asleep, O Lord, to the soul of thy servant departed this life, and *make his memory to be eternal*'. And the choir, in crescendo, responds three times: *Memory eternal! Memory eternal! Memory eternal!*

This preservation of memory through death, which im-plies unbroken consciousness, is always shown to be the pre-requisite for escape from the recurrence of earthly lives. But it is always added that this task is much too hard for unprepared men. Leaving aside the fact that ordinary men are not conscious of themselves *even when alive and in full possession of their senses*, they cannot bear nor can they be expected to bear the tremendous shock of death without the loss of even that awareness they normally possess, any more than ordinary men can be expected to bear great physical pain without fainting. This swooning is inevitable, and part of nature's plan to save men unnecessary suffering, until they can understand its use and value.

Earlier we compared the moment of death, and the escape of the self from a cellular into an electronic state, to an atomic explosion. And it then seemed absolutely clear that such a transition must inevitably involve that black-out of consciousness, which seems recognized in so many legends. As put in the Myth of Er quoted above, 'it was

* κυκλου ταῦ λῆξαι και ἀνάπνευσαι κἄκότητος

necessary that all should drink *a certain measure* of the water'
of forgetfulness. The whole question would then seem—
how soon could the soul struggle out of its insensibility into
awareness of the extraordinary possibilities of the world in
which it found itself? For the reason why most souls fell
into utter oblivion was because '*they that were not preserved
by wisdom drank more than the measure*'.

We thus come to the second reason for loss of memory.
This is connected with the general principle that *change of
state destroys memory*. Our bodies in their summer-state cannot remember their sensations of the winter, nor in the light
of day how they felt in the darkness of the small hours.
A still clearer example is to be seen in the fact that transition
from sleep to waking-state normally destroys the memory of
dreams. Thus only a very special technique of observation
and in particular an intense effort of remembering at the
moment of awakening can enable anything like a consecu-
tive study of dreams to be carried over into day-time consciousness.*

If we regard the tremendous influx of electronic energy at
death as an enormously intensified version of the influx of
light and impressions which occurs at waking, we shall understand why the memory of the past life, after being vividly
illuminated by a first lightning-flash, must inevitably tend
to disappear. Memory of dreams is destroyed on waking,
and memory of life at death, by the same law which causes
metals to lose their power of transmitting sound as soon as
they transmit the more intense energy of heat, or the stars
to disappear in the light of the sun. In order to keep the stars
under observation after dawn, a special and difficult technique of study—from the bottom of a well or with the aid of
screens—is necessary. So it must also be with the retention
of memory through death.

But the carrying over of memory of this life into other
states after death, in order to examine its significance in the
light of conditions there, is only half the problem. For in

* This problem is very well treated in *The Land of Dreams*, by J. G. Sime.

order to make use of such memories, it would be necessary to carry them further still, combined with memories of the invisible worlds, *into the following life*. And to do this a still more formidable change of state must be overcome, namely that connected with birth into the familiar physical world. It is indeed difficult to imagine which would be the greater shock, that resulting from loss of a physical form and formless release into the electronic world at death, or from loss of the womb's protection and release into a world of light, air, noise and cold at birth.

According to Hindu tradition, expressed in the *Vishnu Purana*, it is this latter change of state which most effectively destroys memory:

> The tender and subtle animal exists in the embryo . . . floating in water . . . unable to breathe, endowed with consciousness, and calling to memory many hundred previous births. . . . When the child is about to be born . . . it is turned head downwards, and violently expelled from the womb by the powerful and painful winds of parturition; and the infant, losing for a time all sensation, when brought in contact with the external air is immediately deprived of intellectual knowledge.*

Thus there are two main kinds of memory which we lack and which seem to have been destroyed in rather different ways. In the first place we lack memory of our previous physical lives. This, doubtless, is for the same reason that we lack memory of most of our present life: namely, that it is too painful to recall. In general, *we do not want to remember the past, we prefer to occupy our minds with an imaginary future, quite incompatible with this past. Thus the function of memory atrophies.*

In the second place we have no memory of other states of matter in which we might have existed before conception, nor of the unimaginable freedom and vision belonging to the molecular or electronic worlds. And this, it also seems probable, is because we never learned the special and terribly arduous technique of carrying memory over a fundamental change of being.

* *The Vishnu Purana*, trs. by H. H. Wilson, Book VI, Ch. V, Vol. 5, p. 204

G

Every Soul which is a Man's hath of necessity seen the Things which Verily Are [says Plato in the Phaedrus], else it would not have entered into this creature; but to call Those Things to mind, by means of these, is not easy for every Soul, neither for those Souls which saw the Things there for little space, nor for those unto which, when they were fallen down to Earth, evil happened, so that they are turned to iniquity by evil communications, and forget holy things which they saw aforetime. Verily few are they which are left having Memory present with them in sufficient measure.*

How can memory be developed 'in sufficient measure' for a man to remember himself and carry this remembrance from one world to another, from one life to the next? First he must begin with this present life. For whatever may have happened to the others, this is already photographed within him in every detail, like a film which has been exposed but not developed. Rather there are within him many different films, since each of his functions makes and stores its own record—one reel of all his visual impressions, a second of sounds and conversations he has heard, a third of his own movements, a fourth of physical sensations, and so on. In the cortex of his brain, in his eye, in his throat, the millions of perceptions which make up his life, reduced to molecular or electronic scale, lie dormant but intact.

As we have said, in ordinary man these films are undeveloped, that is, their record is 'forgotten', except when attention is accidentally drawn to this or that short scene by some resemblance or contrast in the present. For it is attention or *consciousness* which is the developing agent. Thus the man who wants to 'develop memory' must bring consciousness intentionally to bear upon his records. He must develop his inner film of the past now, instead of waiting for its sudden and overwhelming revelation at death.

First those memories—of people, places, critical and trivial incidents—which are ordinarily evoked in him only by association, must be brought back sequentially and by will. They must be arranged by months and by years. They must

* *The Myths of Plato*, trs. by J. A. Stewart, p. 319

be assembled, extended, and assessed—*particularly those which he is most reluctant to recall.* For it is exactly the capacity not to remember past weaknesses, embarrassments and failures, which keeps the man as he is, which permits him to repeat the same fatal mistakes constantly and painlessly—or rather to postpone all the resultant suffering of conscience to one last unbearable experience. In this way the first task of a man who wishes to develop memory, is *to remember himself in time.*

But when he seriously tries to do this, he will come across many things in his past, whose repetition he cannot possibly admit. He may find the first trivial manifestation of some habit which later became disastrous; he may recall the first accidental encounter in some fatal relationship; or some foolish negligence which led to a great tragedy. By seeing and facing such memories, he will begin to know himself. He will see what he was—and is. And he will realize that hitherto he only agreed to his past, because he did not remember it.

Studying his own record further, he may see that these dramatic moments of his life, both for good and evil, do not stand alone, but were foreshadowed by many earlier situations, each sketching the coming climax in more complete and circumstantial detail. It may even seem to him that such 'prefigurations' represent a kind of memory *backwards*, the invisible echoing of impulses in reversed time, which we already guessed. And he will realize that for the final scene to be played differently, these 'rehearsals' must also be altered, right back to his very infancy.

From this, there may gradually begin to develop in him a kind of dual memory. He will see at once what actually happened, and *what might have happened, if he had been more conscious.* And the more clearly he remembers the past, the more importance he will attach to these new possibilities, which he will place in a future recurrence. Recurrence will become connected for him with the idea of possible consciousness. *He will begin to reconstruct his life.*

The more he persists in these reconstructions, the more

painful will become the contrast between what was and what might be. And this is a necessary part of the process, for just as consciousness is the developer for the film of memory, so conscience is its fixative. The whole aim must be to develop and fix memory gradually and intentionally, *while still alive*. For just as too strong developer and too violent fixative does not bring out a photograph but irretrievably destroys it, so it is exactly the overwhelming flood of consciousness and conscience released by the electronic state which will *destroy* memory in the moment of death, *unless it has already been developed and permanently fixed during life*.

Thus recalling ever more vividly and keenly the crossroads of his past, the question will arise for a man, how to convey a warning to himself encountering them next time? How to transmit to himself *then* what he feels *now*? Perhaps he may go back to the actual scene of some mistake or opportunity, and striving with all his force to remember himself, endeavour to attach to some wall or tree engraved upon his memory the understanding which he wishes to transmit. He may tell himself that when he stands there *in his next life* the sight of this tree must *remind him to remember*.

It will then be borne in upon him that his only chance is to become conscious *now*. He will understand practically the principle that our only way of communicating memory to another life is by the force of consciousness in this. And he will see that the purpose of acquiring consciousness in life, is *to remain conscious through death*.

XI

SEPARATION BY SUFFERING

PREPARATION for the immense task of remaining conscious through death must be to become intensely conscious of oneself in life. Some principle of consciousness must already have emerged from the body, and have succeeded in studying all the manifestations of this body objectively in the favourable conditions of physical existence, before there can be any question of self-awareness in death. This principle of consciousness must learn *to remember itself*, that is, remember all the manifestations of its physical body and their relation to it, *now*. In no other way can we conceive memory being preserved into another time.

Striving for consciousness in bodily life we are thus in the position of a man adrift in a small boat which has sprung a leak, and who tries to learn to swim while this boat is still afloat, because he knows that it will be too late when it sinks. This power of swimming in another world, this acquisition of a permanent principle of consciousness, is connected with the intentional development of a soul.

Leaving aside for the moment the example of great mystics and religious teachers, we can clearly see that it is this path which has been trodden by many of the greatest writers, artists and musicians, whose secret eludes us if we do not admit such a possibility.

In the work of Shakespeare, for example, we feel a tremendous crescendo of understanding for all the weaknesses, passions, sacrifices, struggles and aspirations of men, which inevitably implies the discovery of all sides of human nature *in himself*, that is, from *self-consciousness*. At the same time, by so vividly seeing and expressing all mortal passions, something in Shakespeare, we feel, has gradually separated itself from them, *remembering all that and yet remaining aside from it*. In Julius Caesar, Macbeth, Hamlet, we see portrayed with many faces this same man who lives through the greatest suffering and tragedy life can bring, and yet in whom something already begins to exist apart from that and apart from his own human feelings in relation to it. It is this very power which gives to all these characters their curious sense of ineffectiveness, when measured by worldly standards. They are already moving on a different path from the rest of humanity: their lives no longer make sense from the point of view of worldly results. *For they are beginning to remember themselves*.

A still more vivid example may be found in the long series of Rembrandt's self-portraits, which, taken together, come as near to portraying the 'long body' of a man as anything in art or literature. From the very earliest, we find Rembrandt striving to 'see himself' and recording, with terrible objectivity, moments of fear, stupidity and uncontrolled mirth when he catches himself with all his guards down and lost in almost bestial unconsciousness.* Gradually, he is able to separate himself from more and more of these human manifestations of Rembrandt, until in the later self-portraits he seems to see *the whole man from outside*. One has an overwhelming impression that recognition has separated itself from the frail humanity, and that Rembrandt knows and remembers himself in a quite different way from ordinary men.

There is another side to the same process. Evidently one of the requirements for escaping certain given conditions of life, certain physical limitations, is that all or most possibilities inherent in those limitations must first be realized. Ordinary men are sentenced to the repetition of their lives because they have not yet begun to become conscious of the possibilities those lives contain. With such men as Rembrandt or Shakespeare the situation is very different. The

* *The Paintings of Rembrandt*, edited by A. Bredius. Nos. 1, 2,3,5,14,15

amount of observation and understanding, relating to every side and situation of human life, to every class and type of human being, which has been wrung out of the material life of Shakespeare, is incalculable.

Repetition is due to lack of understanding. It is the mechanism by which every individual receives another chance to understand more, to become more conscious in his present conditions—since if he cannot master these, it is certain that he will not be able to master other and less familiar ones. But Shakespeare and Rembrandt have already achieved and released immense quantities of understanding from their own lives, and it is thus almost inconceivable that such lives should repeat in the way that unconscious lives must.

For instance, it is impossible to believe that Shakespeare must again write *Hamlet*. He did so once—perfectly. To repeat perfection entails a kind of waste not provided for by cosmic laws. Imperfection repeats, perfection does not. And yet *Hamlet* exists in history. Innumerable performances of it have occupied hundreds of actors and producers, influenced tens of thousands of spectators, created fashions, phrases and trends of thought, which tinge our whole civilization, and have passed even into its most mechanical aspects. Therefore somebody must write *Hamlet*.

In order to escape from recurrence, 'Shakespeare' must teach someone else to write *Hamlet*. He must put someone else in his place. Then he will be free for other tasks. And in fact this example is a good one, for in the famous Bacon-Shakespeare controversy we seem to see the confused trace in ordinary time of the authorship of a great historic work passing from one individual to another in successive recurrences.

How did such men come to their strange position, on the edge of freedom? Their most obvious characteristic is their intense desire to see objectively—*even themselves*. But apart from this we cannot help but be struck by the strange part which suffering seems to play for them. Over and over again we see, entering the lives of such creative geniuses, some great tragedy or suffering which seems strangely inevitable, which they take no trouble to avoid, and which in some curious way they seem to need. It is as if, at a certain point in their growing objectivity towards themselves, no ordinary experience is strong enough, *nothing else but suffering is a sufficient trial of their acquired strength.*

Particularly is this so with such men at the approach of death. Rembrandt, after his magnificent career, died sick, forgotten and absolutely alone. Beethoven, deaf, stricken, helpless and abandoned, was forgotten altogether by the drunken boy sent to fetch a doctor. Tolstoy died at a country railway station when at the age of eighty-two he ran away on an impossible pilgrimage to Tibet. Newton had passed so far beyond ordinary relationships that he was treated as insane; and so was Nietzsche.

Certainly every man's death is tragic and lonely. But in these cases, tragedy and suffering seem to play a quite different rôle from that which they play in the lives of ordinary men. Ordinary men suffer wastefully and uselessly, and for them the endeavour to avoid pointless pain is no doubt right. But already in some of these other cases the quite different element of intentional suffering seems to enter. Suffering is not avoided, and is even sought for, simply because it is the hardest thing for man to deal with, and the greatest test of his acquired power of separating his consciousness from his bodily manifestations and looking down upon these objectively.

When we come to the great religious teachers of humanity, we find such deliberate suffering carried to lengths which from the point of view of ordinary man, are quite incomprehensible. A single word to Pilate could have altered everything. But Christ does nothing whatever to avoid his crucifixion, and indeed acts in such a way—given the circumstances and mood of the people—as to make it inevitable. Socrates before the Athenian senate behaves similarly. The Buddha *knowingly* eats the poisoned food proffered by the blacksmith at a wayside village. While Milarepa, the Tibetan saint, when a jealous pundit promises his mistress a turquoise to give the sage a bowl of poisoned curds, first sends the woman back to get her bribe, and then *deliberately accepts the cup*. In each of these cases it is made clear by the narrators of the story that such wilful death is accompanied by terrible agony, which was clearly foreseen and deliberately invoked.

There must be many meanings of such suffering, most of which remain invisible for us. Yet remember all that has been said about the possibility of escape from the cycle of human lives by carrying full consciousness and memory over death into the moment of release into the electronic world. And how consciousness, to be hardened and tempered to such a test, would have to have proved already its ability to withstand the most terrible shocks and hardships that the physical world could offer.

From one point of view at least the deliberate incurring of great suffering just before death must be to accustom the consciousness to such shocks that it will be able to withstand this final transition without flinching. Mastery of great pain gives consciousness the intensity and 'flight' necessary to continue apart from the body, enables it to 'take off' on its own, so to speak.

For suffering is the chief means by which one part of the human mechanism may be separated from another. Even at the dentist it becomes possible for a man to feel, '*It* suffers, but *I* do not suffer'. Whereas sitting in a comfortable arm-chair in a warm room after a good meal it is practically impossible for him to induce a comparable sensation.

Such division, when carried far, releases tremendous quantities of emotional energy. We now know the immense scale of energy released by the splitting off of electronic shells from the nucleus of the atom. Exactly similar is the release of energy in man by the splitting off of the outer physical shells of his organism from its nucleus, his unknown 'self'. Such splitting is ordinarily produced at death, and the unmanageable results of this uncontrolled fission we have already touched upon.

But, as with the artificial splitting of the atom, so with the artificial separation or loosening of consciousness from the body—the problem is to find a shock violent and penetrating enough to effect the result, while yet keeping the experiment under control.

In the case of man, intense suffering, fully mastered and accurately directed, seems to provide the only shock of necessary intensity. Perhaps the most ecstatic love and compassion could be so used; but in such cases as have been recorded for us, such compassion in fact accepts equivalent suffering, and there appears to be no real difference between the two forces.

Evidently there are grave dangers. The immense shock which results in the splitting of the atom must strike in exactly the right place to knock the electron out of its system. Similarly, in the case of man the application of the great force of suffering exactly between the principle of consciousness and its bodily manifestations, in order to separate the two, is only possible after long moral and psychological preparation. For its wrong application, as in countless sects of flagellants and self-torturers throughout history, may only serve to mutilate the psycho-physical organism and *fuse* the consciousness and the body inseparably together. This, one of the most terrible results of premature experiment, is sufficient warning that everything that has been said *does not refer to ordinary man*. The intentional use of suffering only becomes practical in connection with the work of a *school of regeneration;* and then only at a very definite moment.

For suffering, like heat, is not only a splitting but a fixing agent. It renders possible the loosening and separating of the different sides of man—but it also in some way tends to fuse his fundamental self or individuality indissolubly to that side to which it has gravitated during the actual endurance of pain. Seen from an ordinary point of view its effect is to render permanent those attitudes which were uppermost at the time. The changeability which is both the weakness and salvation of ordinary man is thus lost. So that, as is generally understood, suffering can either destroy or make a man, according to whether he allows his attention to become attached to the unhappy flesh, or whether with a great effort he can transmute it into that principle of consciousness which is able to regard the physical organism and its troubles from a detached and objective point of view.

This terrible *deciding* power of suffering is summarized in the story of the two thieves crucified with Jesus, who, enduring identical pain, one with bitterness and the other with devotion, were, according to popular legend, damned and blessed respectively. In any case Christ's answer to the repentant thief, 'Verily I say unto thee, to-day thou shalt be with me in paradise', suggests the further idea that great suffering, *taken rightly*, may be transmuted into an energy of such intensity as to neutralize all previous records—just as intense heat may melt a bronze tablet and so cause the disappearance of inscriptions apparently engraved thereon for ever.

This possibility of suffering consuming the record of wrong action in the past, which a man can be rid of in no other way; and at the same time of it fixing permanently in him certain characteristics which he feels desirable, but which hitherto have only visited him sporadically, may throw further light on the idea of intentional suffering at the approach of death.

Those men who reached such extraordinary heights of understanding in their different fields, must all have been visited sooner or later by the question: 'How to make permanent such understanding in the face of illness, old age and approaching dissolution?' The artists intuitively and the teachers consciously seem to have come to the same realization—that deliberately chosen suffering may provide exactly such a fixative, that mordant by which the lessons learned in life may be indelibly fixed into the material of man's being. Indeed Milarepa in his pain sings openly:

Diseases . . .
But tend to beautify me greatly . . .
Gifts I use to ornament the signs of my perfection . . .
This illness, which becometh me so well,
I could transfer, but no need is there to do so.*

Two things must however be added here to correct the picture. In the first place, voluntary suffering is only conceivable for him who has long ago freed himself from involuntary suffering—that is, from ordinary worry, fear, apprehension, slavery to others' opinions, imagination of disaster and so on. The only healthy attitude of the man who finds himself at the mercy of such things is a desire to be rid of them as soon as possible, and to place his trust in higher powers. Indeed, to add intentional suffering *on top* of this burden implies an unhealthy and even pathological tendency.

It is only the man who is free of all this who realizes that a new and immense motive force is necessary for what must be done, and who begins to think of the transmutation of pain and discomfort, that one raw material of which human beings have no lack.

Precisely this word 'transmutation' suggests the other qualification we must make to our argument. For 'suffering' is only a description of how certain experiences look to us, from our point of view. If they are in fact only 'suffering', then they have failed in their purpose. But we have every reason to believe that they bring with them joy, ecstasy or some new emotion for which we have no name, in similar or even greater intensity. How then shall we describe a state in which pain and joy are present in equal proportions, or in which physical suffering is accompanied by emotional ecstasy? We have no way of expressing such a state.

'Thou hearest that I suffered, yet did I not suffer; that I suffered not, yet I did suffer; that I was pierced, yet I was not smitten; hanged, and I was not hanged; that blood flowed from me, and it flowed not,' as Christ is made to say

* W. Y. Evans-Wentz: *Tibet's Great Yogi Milarepa*, p. 265

in the apocryphal Acts of John. 'In a word, what they say of me, that befell me not, but what they say not, that did I suffer.'*

*   *   *

Some, *for a special reason*, must be less explicit. After many years devoted to teaching and explaining certain esoteric ideas to his companions, a man I knew, some months before his death, suddenly ceased to explain anything. By almost complete silence and seclusion he seemed to insulate himself, as it were, from the distracting force of life, which sucks the soul out of every man who has not *fixed in himself his own field of consciousness*.

Then in the last month of all, when his death was clearly a matter of days, his weakness extreme, and the severest pain continuous, this man began to undertake without any explanation a series of feats of endurance quite inexplicable from any ordinary point of view. Medically prescribed complete rest, he required to be driven day after day for long excursions across the country to all those houses in which he had lived during his years in England. On these excursions he neither ate nor drank, and on his return would often remain all night sitting in the car in the darkness and cold. When almost unable to set one foot before the other he would make his dying body walk step by step for an hour at a time through the rough lanes; force it to rise in the small hours, dress, descend and climb long flights of stairs; turn night into day; and require of his companions, in order to remain with him, such feats of endurance as they in full possession of health and strength were scarcely able to accomplish.

Finally, on the day which he foresaw as that of his death, he rose from bed, dressed, and by sheer will throwing aside those who wished to restrain him, descended and called about him all his near friends, to whom he was able to

---

* Acts of John, verse 101: *The Apocryphal New Testament*, trs. by Montague Rhodes James, p. 256.

communicate many ideas in such a way that each perceived in them the solution of his own problem. He then retired, and at dawn the next morning knowingly died.

The full meaning of such a performance, either for the man himself or for those about him, must remain unknown to us. It can only be said that with it he demonstrated certain powers, for example speaking to others without audible words and communicating with them at a distance, which are normally regarded as miraculous. And further, that these powers were not exercised for their own sake, but as functions of another state of consciousness, and in relation to some task performed *in another world*.

Suffering belongs to the nature of the physical or organic body. It is his fear of this which binds man to mortality. By intentionally accepting it, he cheats nature and death. He demonstrates the separation of his will from this body's power. He draws apart the soul in readiness for an independent existence in the invisible world. He remembers himself. In such a way man may prepare for conscious immortality.

XII

TRANSFIGURATION
INTO THE ELECTRONIC WORLD

W HAT is the nature of this conscious immortality? First we have to distinguish the possibility of conscious immortality very clearly from *unconscious* immortality. A rock, which lasts ten thousand years in one form, is immortal in relation to man, but its immortality is unconscious. The permanence of hell is a similar immortality.

Thus it is not immortality in itself which is desirable. Indeed to any but the most naïve, there is something inexpressibly horrible about the idea of immortality connected with our present body or our present state of near-unconsciousness. For this would mean the end of all possibilities of change, of growth, of development. Unconscious immortality implies the freezing or petrifaction of *one* form; it is the quality of a form which is *unable to die*. Conscious immortality is connected with the power of passing freely from one form to another, of transcending lower forms for higher. It is the quality of a life-principle which has become *independent of dying forms*. These two possibilities are the antitheses of one another.

Now the power of changing from one form or vehicle to another implied in conscious immortality depends on a very definite principle. In order to become consciously immortal in one world—that is, to acquire the power of changing one's vehicle in that world at will—it is necessary both to possess and control a body belonging to the world above, a body of the next finer state of matter.

We may take a very simple example of this principle. Houses, buses, aeroplanes, railway trains are vehicles made from matter in mineral state. Physical man possesses the power to change at will from one such vehicle to another through his full control over a cellular body, a body made of matter in a higher state. If his car or his house 'dies', that is, decays or fails to function, he can abandon it and acquire a new one. Thus in a certain sense physical man can be said to be immortal in relation to these vehicles. For he can enter, inhabit, leave or change them at will.

The same cellular body makes him also omnipotent in relation to matter in mineral or metallic state. He can fashion objects from such matter, melt them down, re-form them into new objects, and so on. In relation to a piece of iron or the vehicles made from it he is both immortal and omnipotent; he is 'god'.

We can now understand why the idea of becoming truly immortal in relation to the cellular world is only conceivable in connection with the creation of a higher body, that is, a soul, and with full control over all its powers. To think of purely physical man acquiring immortality and omnipotence in the cellular world would be like imagining that a bicycle could acquire control over other vehicles on its own level.

It follows from all this that there are inherent in the universe many degrees of immortality. Each world of matter is immortal in relation to the denser world below. The molecular world of earth is immortal in relation to the cellular world of nature, which periodically dies and is reborn upon its surface. The electronic or solar world of light is immortal in relation to the molecular world of earth. And a being possessing a body of the nature and matter of one such world must enjoy potential immortality in relation to beings inhabiting the world below.

Thus if a man having full control over a cellular body is immortal and omnipotent in the world of mineral bodies, a man having full control over a molecular body or soul may in turn be immortal and omnipotent in the world of cellular bodies. And a man having full control over an electronic body or spirit will be immortal and omnipotent in the world of molecular bodies—that is, *he will be immortal and omnipotent in the world of men's souls.*

Now at last we begin to grasp the immense significance of a spirit. For a man who has been able to live in a permanent body of this divine energy which to ordinary men comes only as a lightning-flash at death, will be a *maker of men's souls.* He will be able to work, construct, form and destroy in relation to molecular matter, as physical man is able in relation to mineral matter. He will be able to know and use the laws governing molecular bodies, and he will thus be able *to fashion souls for men, or help them to fashion souls for themselves.*

When we spoke earlier about the possibility of men acquiring souls, we had then to add that no one stage in this process could they expect to accomplish unaided. Now it is clear why. When we find a mineral vessel or utensil—say a buried jar or pot—we immediately conclude the intervention of physical man. In the same way we cannot imagine a formed and *fully-functioning* physical body without the intervention of soul, nor a formed and fully-functioning soul without the intervention of spirit.

We thus begin to distinguish three distinct stages in the possible development of man from his present possession of a physical body, only partly conscious and largely uncontrolled.

First he must find a man who has acquired a soul or molecular body. For only such a man will be omnipotent in relation to physical bodies. Only such a man will understand the laws referring to cellular bodies, be able to diagnose deficiencies or abnormalities, prescribe the very complicated series of exercises and shocks, physical, mental and emotional, necessary to build up nervous strength, break down inner and outer habits, and render the cellular body normal, controlled, sensitive and fully-functioning. The true work of a man with soul will thus be to *reform* physical men, *to make them normal.* He may conduct a 'school of

H

normality'. For it is a principle that only the normal can develop, only the normal can become supernormal.

In addition, he may perhaps teach his pupils the theory of acquiring a soul. He may help them to develop the will, awareness, unity and conscience which we have seen to be essential to this tremendous task. But he will not be able to endow them with souls: he will be unable to work directly in the molecular world.

Only a man who himself lives in the *spirit* will be able to form and fashion souls; as the man with a soul could form and fashion bodies. Such a one will work with men who have already succeeded in becoming physically normal and in whom embryonic souls have begun to grow; and he may form, develop and educate these souls. He may conduct a 'school of souls', about the conditions and circumstances of which we can have little idea.

Finally, we have to suppose schools for the achievement of spirit, concerning whose conduct and work we cannot even theorize. 'I baptise you with water unto repentence; but he that cometh after me is mightier than I . . . He shall baptise you with the Holy Spirit and with fire,'* as John the Baptist says. Water refers to soul: fire to spirit.

Only one aspect of such schools is conceivable to us, and concerns us. A candidate must already possess a mature soul. And the acquisition of spirit by such a man may be connected with the possibility of his endowing his own pupils with the soul he already possesses. This will be his test. *He must put someone in his place.*

This idea reveals to us one of the chief principles connected with the creation of new bodies, and consequent change of place in the universe. And it also reveals why this task is so extraordinarily difficult. As all our study has gone to show, the entire universe is solid; it is a complete whole formed by the recurrence of everything in its own place. So that for one object 'to leave its place'—say for a man to leave his place in the cellular world and acquire a

* St. Matthew III. 11

permanent place in the molecular world—two things are necessary. First, some place in the molecular world must be vacated, *in order to make room for him*. And second, some man from a lower level of understanding must step into the place he himself vacates. Further, although we cannot imagine how, this process must continue out of sight both above and below. A whole chain of men must move, each into the other's place. Only thus can real change of place occur, without leaving some place in the universe empty, that is, without creating an impossible vacuum.

It is now clear why the transfer of human consciousness to a permanent body of higher matter is radically different from every other task open to man. For this, and this alone, implies change of cosmic place. We have to realize that every ordinary kind of 'improvement' known—every form of training and learning, the acquisition of new knowledge, good habits, skills, crafts, even the improvement of being itself—refers to improvement in the same place.

An engine may be cleaned, oiled, painted, accelerated, it may be transferred from driving a concrete-mixer to making electric light—but it still remains the same engine. All this is improvement in the same place. For the engine to breathe, sense, produce young and acquire cellular structure would mean a change from one place in the universe to another. And it is to change of this nature that the creation of new bodies refers.

Now such a chain-movement upwards into higher matter, such a convulsive upheaval of consciousness, creating as it were a vertical split through so many realms, is an extraordinarily complicated process. It needs countless favourable circumstances, individual, cosmic, and even social. In the first place it is only possible in connection with the work of a school conducted by a man who has full command over all the powers of the soul, and who is urgently aspiring to a higher level. Secondly, it is only possible at one certain moment in the history of that school, a moment for which all the school's previous work was but preparation.

Indeed, if we think of the countless tests on many different levels which will have to be taken, the opportunities of moral and physical suffering that must be invented, the variety of types, the different levels of being, the dramatic situations necessary—all of which must be introduced *intentionally*, with full knowledge of their relation to the outcome —then we see that nothing short of a tremendous *cosmic drama* must be produced. Someone must produce a play— *in life*, and in which all the dangers, threats, tortures, ransoms, escapes and deaths are *actual historical events*.

Early on we realized that by the arrangement of the universe the moment of death is the greatest test and opportunity which comes to man. For in this moment *everything is possible*. If then it is the aim of the leader of the school to achieve spirit, with all that that implies, we have to suppose that after intense preparation he will choose the moment of his own death to make this supreme effort. The plot of the drama, its chief event, will be *the death of the producer*.

At the same time, the circumstances of this death, the sacrifices, sufferings, efforts and betrayals which lead up to it, will provide innumerable tests or sub-plots affecting every character within the sphere of the play. They will provide one series of tests for the leader's 'disciples', whose own aim may be to achieve souls; another series for the understanding of ordinary men who may happen to be servants or shopkeepers or bystanders; a third series for public characters of the time; and perhaps a fourth or final chance of redemption for criminals or 'dying souls' whose participation may be necessary to the plot.

How can a coherent and intensely purposeful play be produced with such a heterogeneous collection of characters? When actual saints, murderers, traitors and redeemers have each to play their parts exactly, how can the manifold action be directed to a foreseen end? It is impossible, save by the special function of *telepathy*. Only a man with the power of placing thoughts and suggestions directly in other men's minds can produce such a play. This power is a function of the soul, which by reason of its molecular structure, *can enter into other men and know what is going on in their brains and other organs*. Thus the producer of such a play can only be one who has already acquired a soul and full control over it, and who in connection with his own death is attempting to establish himself in a permanent electronic body or spirit.

This 'telepathic' production of itself sorts out and tests the various characters in the play. The first test will be whether those so directed recognize what is happening to them. Suppose the suggestion of some familiar action to be put into a man's mind. He will certainly take this for his own thought, and if he is not too lazy or too busy he will probably carry out the suggestion, saying that he *decided to do that*. On the other hand, if the suggestion refers to an unfamiliar or un-characteristic action, he will—unless very deeply moved by emotion—set it aside, with the explanation to himself that he *decided not to*. Thus all the ordinary characters in such a play can be used to do what they usually do; they will play their natural rôles, *but as the action requires*.

For the 'disciples', however, the situation is different. Finding the image of very difficult or uncharacteristic actions in their mind, if they have been used to school discipline and to serious inner struggle for self-mastery, they may see these as a special *opportunity* and do their best to perform them. Suppose some great self-sacrifice or defiance of convention for the sake of their loyalty is suggested to them. The weak disciple will set it aside, saying to himself: 'After all the leader never told me to do so.' The strong disciple on the other hand may see a chance of developing will, of mastering his own weakness.

Further, if he has learned to know himself very well, he may recognize that such thoughts are uncharacteristic of him, that they *could not spring from his habitual mind*. He may perhaps connect them with conscience, or if he is very observant he may even suspect their true origin and begin to guess what is happening. In any case, he will say to himself that they must come from a *higher level* and cannot be ignored.

In this way the possibility comes to such disciples to break their own mechanicalness of action, to act out of character. They are enabled to do what they could never even imagine unaided, and yet do it *of themselves, of their own volition*. The effect of this on the disciple is quite different from that of similar actions performed out of obedience, and cannot be simulated in any other way. Thus by true telepathy the disciple is given a chance to surpass himself, to develop will, and to create a soul.

It need hardly be added that no wrong actions can be suggested in such a play. Such actions, which are in one sense required by the plot, are *automatically* provided by the weakness of various characters when confronted with certain key situations. The power-loving man, when his power is threatened, must connive to kill: no suggestion is necessary. Even the disciples, when some turn in the action takes them off their guard, will betray out of timorousness or embarrassment, as did Peter at the cockcrow. The crowd will roar for blood this time, simply because it did a thousand times before. Such actions are absolutely mechanical and *never* the result of the producer's suggestion, though they will certainly be foreseen and taken into account by him. It may even happen that, knowing a disciple's chief weakness, the producer may create some external situation calculated to bring out this weakness almost irresistibly, while *at the same time suggesting to the disciple telepathically how he may overcome it*. In this way may be produced the tremendous inner friction necessary to acquire a soul.

A few 'scenarios' of such plays have come down to us, preserved in the mass of more philosophical scripture. How many unrecorded productions have taken place, and how many have not yet passed beyond the stage of preliminary rehearsals we can never know. For although these dramas may take place openly, it is a strange fact that no record of them ever persists, except that consciously composed and given out. If the producers are not yet ready to record, the performance remains unknown.

Perhaps the clearest recordings centre round the figures of Buddha, of Milarepa, and of Christ. The Buddhist account known as the *Book of the Great Decease* appears to be very incomplete, and to have been edited and formalized till almost all the spontaneity of an *actual* living performance has disappeared. The final episodes of the life of Milarepa, on the contrary, are very lifelike and contain some interesting variants on the Christian drama. But it is this latter, the Gospel, which must represent the perfect example—the classical performance as it were—of such a play.

There are certain other differences. For various reasons both Buddha and Milarepa produced their dramas against a 'sympathetic' scene, in countries where occult ideas were highly revered, and at periods when perhaps for cosmic reasons ordinary men found themselves in an unusually receptive mood. The background of Christ's drama is much more familiar. The strategic outpost of a great bureaucratic empire, nervous officials and an irresponsible mob, political oppression and the shadow of revolt—all this is by no means 'sympathetic'. Yet it shows that the possibility of a general 'move' in level of consciousness, which may in the end affect hundreds of thousands or millions of men, does not at all depend on conditions that from an ordinary point of view we would call favourable. The familiar evil of life may even be 'used', as a kind of fulcrum, to give higher forces a purchase against which to work and attain their ends.

Despite such differences of scene, the types of such a drama appear permanent. The Roman centurion who suddenly sees through the political crucifixion to burst out, 'Truly this man was the Son of God!' *is the same character* as Socrates' jailer who, bringing the poison, begs forgiveness of 'the noblest and gentlest and best of all who ever came to this place.'

At the same time, each role may be played with individual differences depending on the particular actor and the particular production. The innkeeper who serves Buddha the

rotten food from which he dies is introduced as a quite
minor character, whose critical action is almost 'accident'.
In the Christian drama, on the other hand, Judas is taken
as the personification of evil, and though he finally repents,
is still required to hang himself. Even here, however, there
is a curious suggestion of collusion at the Last Supper and
in Christ's phrase at the betrayal: 'Friend, wherefore art
thou come?' And the role is given a new turn altogether in
the drama of Milarepa, where the jealous pundit, after pro-
curing the poisoning of the saint, ironically asks to receive
the resulting agony, and having a small part of it transferred
to him, is converted, abandons his wealth, and becomes a
devout disciple. Here is an example of how an outwardly
villainous role can be played in such a way as to prepare the
actor for quite a different role *next time*.

For we have to accept the idea that in all such dramas,
each conscious actor must eventually learn to play all parts,
with the idea that he may one day even qualify for the cen-
tral role itself. In the Gospel drama, for example, there are
many hints that Saint John—'the disciple whom Jesus loved',
who alone stayed with him at the crucifixion, to whose
care he entrusted his mother, whose gospel reveals the
deepest emotional understanding, and above all, who later
as an old man in Patmos himself described the experiences
of an electronic body—was, so to speak, 'understudying the
Christ'. 'The imitation of Christ' is in fact the ultimate task
of every player in the Christian mystery.

All such parts, however, are but subsidiary. For the real
significance of the whole play must lie in *the transfiguration of
the chief character into the electronic world*, his achievement of
spirit. And all the miraculous events and manifestations
which follow his death may in one sense be seen as a demon-
stration that *the play has succeeded*, the tremendous miracle
has been accomplished.

For the colossal shifting of place through all levels o
matter, the vertical split through the whole universe, which
is necessary to this transfiguration, seems to reverberate

not only up to heaven but down into the mineral world, to hell itself.

At his passing, Jetsün exhibited the process of merging the physical body with the Realm of Eternal Truth. . . . The unclouded sky appeared as if it were palpable with prismatic colours. . . . There were profuse showers of blossoms. . . . Ravishingly melodious music . . . and a delicious perfume, more fragrant than any earthly essence, pervaded the air. . . . Gods and men met and conversed . . . so that, for the time being, they were carried back to the Golden Age.*

When [Buddha] the Exalted One died there arose, at the moment of his passing out of existence, a mighty earthquake, terrible and awe-inspiring: and the thunders of heaven burst forth.†

Jesus, when he had cried again with a loud voice, yielded up the ghost. And behold the veil of the temple [time] was rent in twain from the top to the bottom; and the earth did quake, and the rocks rent; and the graves were opened; and many bodies of the saints which slept arose, and came out of the graves after his resurrection, and went into the holy city, and appeared unto many.‡

All this confirms the idea that some tremendous birth-pang, involving all parts of the universe, has taken place. A crack has been produced through all levels of matter, and through time itself by the direct intervention of electronic energy. Through this crack the perception of ordinary men may for a short time see into higher worlds and into the past and future. And through it, for all beings, there now lies a way of escape which did not exist before.

Thereafter, a different category of miracles takes place. Nearly all the miracles attributed to Christ during his life refer to the healing or making normal of the physical body. The healing of the nobleman's son at Capernaum, of the cripple at the pool of Bethesda, of the ten lepers, of the blind man and the woman with an issue of blood, all refer to adjustments of physical nature, such as we might expect from a man who enjoyed complete control over the functions of a molecular body, and whose work was to create 'normal men'.

* W. Y. Evans-Wentz: *Tibet's Great Yogi Milarepa*, pp. 273-4
† 'The Book of the Great Decease', Ch. VI, v. 10, trs. by T. W. and C. A. F. Rhys Davids, *Dialogues of the Buddha*, Part 2.　　　‡ St. Matthew, xxvii. 50-3

The miracles after the crucifixion, however, are of a different order. Christ was then able to project a *new* physical body, or many such bodies, in different places, *after his original body had been destroyed*. Suddenly two friends, walking in the country to Emmaus, find a physical Christ beside them: the same day another Christ appears to disciples inside a locked room: a week later there is another appearance to Thomas under similar conditions: while a fourth Christ comes to disciples fishing, across the Lake of Tiberias. In each case, a very curious proof of physical existence is made *by the appearing Christ himself*, who insists upon eating food or upon being touched. This would seem curiously irrelevant, were its aim not to show that the appearance is no hallucination, even no vision, *but an actual physical body*. For to those who understood, this alone would be proof that Christ had reached a realm where he could create and destroy bodies at will, that is, he had complete freedom of all vehicles, and was working *in the spirit from the electronic world*.

So also, preparing for death and begged by different disciples to do so at their various villages, Milarepa accompanies them all and remains with all who stay behind.

Such proof of the power to pass freely from one body to another, which belongs to conscious immortality, will be one of the greatest tests of the teacher's disciples and must produce consternation and terror among those who have not yet guessed what lies at stake. Milarepa's followers begin to quarrel among themselves, each claiming that since they were with the teacher the others could not have been. In the end he himself must intervene: 'All of you are right. It is I who was playing with you.'

So when Mary Magdalene and the two pilgrims to Emmaus, beside themselves with their experience, hurry back to tell the meeting of 'official disciples' in Jerusalem, they are treated as insane. 'And they believed them not.' For it is one of the strangest ironies that the most bitter disbelievers in the teacher's transfiguration must be found among those who were most familiar with him in the guise of ordinary man. Some must always deny his spirit in the name of his physical body: for their memories of the man will seem real, the miracle imagination.

This disbelief in the great experiment, *exactly because it has succeeded*, is among the strangest and most incomprehensible results of the drama. And we have to realize how naïve is the ordinary man's idea that a miracle would make him believe. If a man has scepticism in him, a miracle will certainly *make him disbelieve*. For finding himself utterly unable to produce a reasonable explanation, he must come to the conclusion that either himself or his teacher has gone mad. And if he cannot transcend his ordinary attitudes and ideas, the very miracle may cut him off from his teacher; perhaps forever.

Thus this moment of miracles, this dénouement of the drama, brings perhaps the greatest test of all. The disciples may have passed many other tests, made great efforts, and understood much. Now all depends whether they have *positive attitude*, or in religious language faith, towards their teacher. For only with complete faith and purged of fear can they follow him to the electronic world.

Yet for those who pass this test, a quite new connection with their teacher becomes possible. For by virtue of his electronic body he can reach them anywhere and at any time. By the nature of electronic matter, which penetrates all things, he can possess them and make them do his will, as long as they so wish. By the nature of electronic matter, which surpasses time, he can come to them in the future, and perhaps even in the past. He has become not only omnipotent but eternal in relation to them. And he can exercise his power of creating souls, not only among them, but among all men who believe in him, as long as electronic matter endures. His indeed will be *conscious immortality*.

'Lo, I am with you alway, even unto the end of the world.'

*   *   *

Of my own teacher I can only say that he also produced among his friends a play, of which they unwittingly but perfectly played their parts, and whose plot was his own death. Silent, he instructed them in their hearts, some recognizing and some not. 'I will always be with you', he too could say —but lightly and smoking a cigarette, so that none noticed. Lying in bed in Surrey, he possessed with his own mind a young man flying over the Atlantic, whom he had already rid of an illusion. That morning dead, he walked with a traveller—crossing London Bridge; and to another at the wheel of a car showed the nature of the universe.

Yet these tales are hard to believe. Of his achievement then let this present book stand witness, written this year following his death, of knowledge undeserved by me. Let him who can understand understand. For so it is.

November 19, 1948

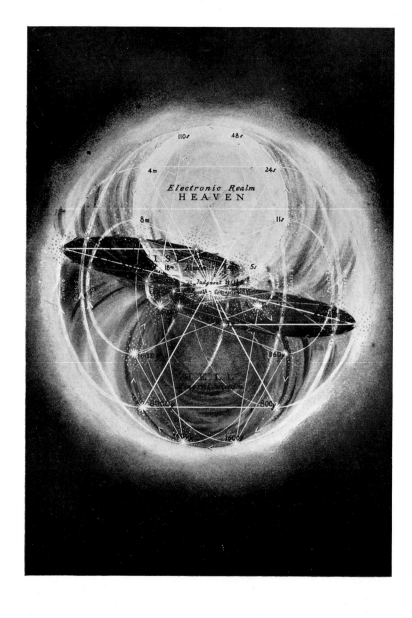

APPENDIX

A MODEL OF THE UNIVERSE

SUPPOSE our figure of four conjoined circles to represent the worlds and times of *matter in mineral state*, *matter in cellular state*, *matter in molecular state*, and *matter in electronic state*. Using this figure as a kind of 'philosophical machine', we can reproduce in symbolic form many interesting aspects of the universe. At the same time these particular definitions probably make it unsuitable for the study of phenomena beyond the limits of the solar system.

The circumference of each of the circles is marked by a time-scale developing logarithmically in three stages. We established the circle of mineral life to have a scale ranging from 80,000 to 8000 to 800 to 80 years, appropriate to the measurement of processes passing inside the crust of the earth, in a realm symbolically represented by ancient ideas of 'hell'. The circle of cellular life similarly extends from 80 years to 1 month and is appropriate to the lives and processes of organic beings on the earth's surface, or simply on 'earth'. The circle of molecular life extends from 1 month to 40 minutes and measures lives and phenomena belonging to the terrestrial atmosphere, or in old terminology to 'paradise'. The circle of electronic life extends from 40 minutes to $2\frac{1}{2}$ seconds and refers to the phenomena of light, depending upon the sun in 'heaven'.

In this way the four circles straightened out represent a continuous scale of lifetimes ranging from 80,000 years to $2\frac{1}{2}$ seconds, or a range of speed of experience of one million million times.

Thus from one point of view the four circles can be taken to represent the mineral world, the organic world, the molecular world and the electronic world, or the four ancient 'worlds' of hell, earth, paradise and heaven. While from another point of view they represent the passage of the individual lives through these four worlds, the relative speed of motion in them.

When we studied the circle of human life, which has now become the typical pattern of the world of cellular bodies, we realized that at birth (10 months) and at the end of childhood (8 years), as well as at the single point of death and conception (80 years), there entered some direct impulse of creative force, some completely new potentiality from the origin of life. These points mark the three stages of logarithmic progression referred to. Thus in this circle—as also in the three others—we may join these points by a triangle which will represent the direct intervention of solar or divine energy in each world. These triangles radiate into all worlds from their single point of conjunction, the point of death-conception common to all worlds, the point of universal judgment. This point, whence all lives derive, to which they return, and which sustains them in their circling, is the sun itself. These triangles of solar radiation must be seen as in constant motion, and this *first motion* will represent *life*.

Next, the six intermediate points or milestones on each circle may be taken, like the planets within the solar system, to indicate 'functions' or 'organs' of their respective worlds. Between them passes an internal circulation of energy, transmitted or reflected from one to the other in a certain pattern, as a ray of light might pass eternally between a series of reflecting mirrors appropriately placed. From this circulation, or 'play of lights', which constitutes the *second motion* of the universe, is created the whole variety of *form* appropriate to the world in question.

We have therefore to imagine the four circles of mineral, cellular, molecular and electronic life as each irradiated by a moving triangle of divine energy, and each informed by an inner circulation of its own.

Further, we have to imagine the corresponding points in the circles of the different worlds to be themselves connected by the passage of certain influences from one world to another—as birth in the cellular world must in some unknown way be controlled by birth in the molecular and electronic worlds, or as a planet may influence a corresponding organ of the human body. This influencing of a function of one world by the similar function of another is the *third motion* of the universe, which is expressed by the law '*as above, so below*'.

These three motions between them form the static solid of the universe. And they create from their interplay the lives which pass round the circles of the worlds, at speeds appropriate to the resistance of each medium. Thus the quantum of energy inherent in the original impulse of an individual life must pass through the cellular world at one speed, through the greatly decreased resistance of the molecular world at a much higher speed, and through the tremendous resistance of the mineral world a thousand times more slowly.

The passage of lives round the circles of worlds introduces the *fourth motion* of the universe, the fourth dimension, that is, *time*.

Looking at our model of the universe, we have therefore to begin by imagining four kinds of movement in it. First, the movement of divine radiation round each of the triangles; second, the movement of inner circulation between the six intermediate points in each world; third, the movement from each point in one circle to the corresponding points in other circles; and fourth, the movement of lives round the different circles themselves.

But the purpose of this 'philosophical machine' is to help us create the image of six motions, a universe of six dimensions. We have therefore to set the whole structure in motion in two more ways.

For the sake of distinction let us imagine the circle of the mineral world coloured red, the circle of the cellular world green, the circle of the molecular world blue, and the circle of the electronic world yellow or gold.

Now let us imagine the whole structure suspended from the outermost point of the electronic or golden circle, and revolving rapidly upon itself. A very curious but interesting figure will appear. This will resemble a large sphere or bubble, in the upper half of which is contained a smaller sphere or bubble of gold, and in the lower an equal sphere or bubble of red, the two separated by a green diaphragm created by the horizontal motion of the blue and green circles of molecular and cellular life. In the gold electronic sphere both the triangle and the inner figure will be clearly visible as they will also be visible in the red mineral sphere below. The flat motion of the blue and green circles, however, has produced nothing but a green film, in which both triangle and inner figure have completely disappeared.

Here we have a very beautiful image of the universe as we perceive it, that is, of the differentiation of worlds. The gold sphere represents the sphere of full solar light or electronic life *above* the surface of the earth, in which the operation of both sun and planets is apparent even to our perception. The red sphere represents the sphere of minerals *below* the surface of the earth. While the green disc or film represents the sphere of organic life *on* the earth's surface, created by the interpenetration of the cellular and molecular worlds, and in which the operation of divine laws is as it were hidden by its very complexity, by the shimmer of its many motions.

Several aspects of our universe are conveyed by this motion, the fifth motion of our figure. We perceive that heaven and hell are separated by a film without thickness— the plane of the earth's surface, the plane of interpenetration of earth and paradise. In this plane both the upper electronic sphere and the lower mineral sphere are adjacent and visible. But seen from above or from heaven it is this terrestrial surface which renders invisible its mineral interior, just as it

renders the heaven-world invisible from below. From another point of view the whole large bubble may be taken as
symbol of the universal illusion or *maya*.

Such is our *fifth motion*, the world of the fifth dimension in
which an image of the universe is created by the *eternal
recurrence* or revolution of all things in their own place.

To obtain a sixth motion, we must imagine the four
circles spinning about their meeting-point. The figure will
now assume a form resembling a full chrysanthemum, white
in colour. Observing it, we realize that both the triangle
and the figure of inner circulation have become continuous,
that is *one:* and further, that the colours of the four worlds
have combined to produce white or colourlessness. This
means that in their spinning all four worlds exist at all points,
that is, they completely interpenetrate one another. With
this motion the figure represents the interpenetration of
worlds, the state of a body simultaneously composed of mineral, cellular, molecular and electronic matter, the idea that
everything is everywhere. In this motion, the *sixth*, *all
possibilities are realized*.

Remembering all that we have put together about the significance of the different circles, of the movements within
the different circles, of the movement of the circles, and of
the movements of the whole figure, we must try to combine
these last two motions, and imagine to ourselves a figure in
which *all six motions are proceeding simultaneously*. Such a
figure will probably represent the nearest approach to a
correct model of the universe possible to the purely logical
mind.*

*   *   *

It may be asked why the time-scale which passes round
the circles or through the four worlds should have definite
limits of $2\frac{1}{2}$ seconds at one end and 80,000 years at the other.
What is the meaning of the fact that individual duration

* Compare the figure of Van Manen's vision, quoted in Ouspensky's *Tertium
Organum*, p. 133

I

longer than 80,000 years or shorter than 2½ seconds is outside our figure? Why not a fifth or sixth circle?

Apparently our figure of the four states of matter, interpreted in this way, pictures the universe as far as it concerns the actual possibilities of individual beings on earth. It is a model of the universe as seen from this place.

For if we try to conceive a fifth circle, where conception was at 80,000 years, birth at 800,000 years, where maturity began at 8,000,000 years, and where the full term of life was 80,000,000 years, we find ourselves unable to fit such appalling slowness of development into earthly conditions.

According to our scale of cellular life the embryo of man already loses half its speed at point 1 of its circle, that is, at two months. In the same way it has been established that radium, one of the densest matters known and which evidently belongs not to the surface but to the interior of the earth, loses half its radio-activity, half its speed, in 1600 years. But a being conceived into this fifth circle, were it to exist, would only lose half its initial momentum in 160,000 years. It would live a hundred times more slowly than radium.

We can think only of one place where such conditions could obtain—that is, upon the moon. There, as we said, *no change* has been apparent in the few thousand years of recorded human observation. So that certainly we can only conceive of serious change occurring on the moon in periods of hundreds of thousands or millions of years. Thus the fifth circle of time, referring to matter in a lower state than mineral, if we can suppose it to refer to anything, probably refers to life conditions on the moon. These do not concern us, do not enter into the possible experience of beings upon earth at all, and if we can conceive of earthly beings descending into such a circle, it is clear that they could never return. For they would have gone outside the earthly universe with its four states of matter altogether.

In the same way beings who lived in a higher state of matter than the electronic would also have gone beyond the sphere of earthly beings—for they would live in a higher medium than solar energy, that is, they would have become independent of the sun and free of the Milky Way.

It is for this reason that, however we may try, we cannot introduce a fifth circle into this model of *our universe*.

BIBLIOGRAPHY

(*a*) Original Texts

Aeneid of Virgil: trs. by H. Rushton Fairclough. London, 1942.

Apocryphal New Testament: trs. by Montague Rhodes James. Oxford, 1945.

Bible: Old and New Testaments.

Bhagavadgita: *The Song of God*, trs. by Swāmi Prabhavananda and Christopher Isherwood. London. 1947.

Book of the Craft of Dying: trs. by Frances M. M. Comper. London, 1917.

Buddha: 'The Book of the Great Decease', trs. by T. W. and C. A. F. Rhys Davids ('*Dialogues of the Buddha*', part 2). London, 1910.

Divine Comedy of Dante Alighieri.

Egypt: *The Book of the Dead*, trs. by Sir E. A. Wallis Budge. London, 1923.

Heaven and Hell of Swedenborg: trs. by Rev. James Robson Rendell. London, 1937.

Heracleitus: '*On the Universe*', trs. by W. H. S. Jones. London, 1931.

Hermetica: trs. by Walter Scott. Oxford, 1924.

Plato, The Myths of: trs. by J. A. Stewart, London. 1905.

Tibetan Book of the Dead: trs. by Lāma Kazi Dawa-Samdup and W. Y. Evans-Wentz. O.U.P., 1927.

Tibet's Great Yogi Milarepa: trs. by Lāma Kazi Dawa-Samdup and W. Y. Evans-Wentz. Oxford, 1928.

Tibetan Yoga and Secret Doctrine: trs. by Lāma Kazi Dawa-Samdup and W. Y. Evans-Wentz. Oxford, 1935.

Upanishads, The Ten Principal: trs. by Shree Purohit Swāmi and W. B. Yeats. Faber and Faber Ltd., London, 1937.

Vishnu Purana: trs. by H. H. Wilson and Fitzedward Hall. London, 1864.

Zoroastrian Doctrine of a Future Life: by Jal Dastur Cursetji Pavry. New York, 1929.

(*b*) Modern Books

Adams, W. Marsham: *The House of the Hidden Places*. London, 1895.

Brahmacari, Srimad Vivekaprasada: *A Samkhya Catechism*. Madhupur, 1935.

Bredius, A. (edited by): *The Paintings of Rembrandt*. Vienna, 1937.

Budge, Sir E. A. Wallis: *Egyptian Ideas of the Future Life*. London, 1900.

Flammarion, Camille: *Death and its Mystery*. London.

Ibsen, Henrik: *Peer Gynt*, trs. by Norman Ginsbury. London, 1945.
Kondakov, Nikodim Pavlovich: *The Russian Icon*, trs. by Ellis H. Minns. Oxford, 1927.
Ouspensky, P. D.: *A New Model of the Universe*. London, 1934.
Ouspensky, P. D.: *Strange Life of Ivan Osokin*. New York, 1947.
Phaidon Press: *The Paintings of El Greco*. London, 1938.
Sime, J. G.: *The Land of Dreams*. Toronto, 1940.

THE ILLUSTRATIONS

PLATE I TIBETAN CIRCLE OF LIFE (BHAVACHAKRA)

Round the outside of the circle develop inevitably the stages of life in time, from conception to birth, marriage, maturity, death and rebirth again. The six compartments within the circle represent the various states of existence—the Heaven World, the World of Demigods or Paradise, the World of Unhappy Ghosts or Purgatory, the Hell World, the Animal World, and the Human World—all within the circle of time, and into any of which the dying man may enter in the fateful moment of judgment. In the inner circle is shown the rising and falling of human souls: and in the centre the cock, snake and pig, symbolizing the triad of Lust, Anger and Ignorance which keeps the Universe or Samsara in motion. The dragon which sustains the whole is the momentum of life, beyond which lie timelessness and unity.

Reproduced by courtesy of Mrs Antoinette K. Gordon

PLATE II   MADONNA OF THE CIRCLES

The Madonna, as the Milky Way, bears and displays the Christ of the Sun. From him spring and to him eternally return the circle of physical life, weighed down by the Moon, and the circle of invisible life ascending to the stars.

PLATE III AZTEC JUDGMENT (TONALAMATL OR SACRED CALENDAR OF
THE CODEX BORBONICUS)

Man climbs the tree of life between Tonatiuh, Lord of the Sun and Life, and Mictlan-
tecuhtli, Lord of the Underworld and Death. Around the root of the tree, which
grows from symbols representing earth, air, fire and water, are assembled the constituent parts which came together at his conception—the fertilized seed, the hog of personality, the hawk of spirit, and the wings of his soul in a basket spangled with stars.

At the height of the tree, or death, shines the symbol of the sun itself, from which
radiate four rays or paths. Thence spring the wings of the soul, released at last.
While above, his various parts, split asunder by death, go to their destinies—to the
left or side of death the corpse tied in its shroud, and the beast which returns to the
root of the tree: to the right or side of life the serpent, principle of consciousness,
which came from the sun, and the spirit by which man is transfigured into the starry
world.

Above all broods the Milky Way of countless suns.

PLATE IV   EGYPTIAN JUDGMENT (PAPYRUS OF ANI, 15TH CENTURY B.C.)

Under the assembled company of gods, the soul of the scribe Ani enters the Hall of Judgment. His heart, or acquired being, is weighed by Anubis, against the feather of Maät, his possibility. Thoth displays the tablet bearing the record of his life, and Ammet, devourer of the unjustified, lies in wait. His soul, hawk-winged, is poised above; his luck or destiny stands below; while the unshapen block of his future embryo—attended by the twin goddesses of birth—await the impress of the body which will be awarded to him by the Judgment.

After, Ani, justified by the Judgment, is led by Horus into the presence of Osiris, where—transfigured—he appears radiant as the sun and with a solar disc rising from his crown. And before Osiris, upon a lotus, already stand the Children of Horus, the Inner Circle of Humanity.

Reproduced by permission of the Trustees of the British Museum

PLATE V RUSSIAN JUDGMENT (IKON OF THE SECOND DREAD COMING
OF CHRIST)

Watched by the multitudes of all humanity, past and present, ignorant and righteous, and interceded for before Christ by Adam and Eve, the soul is weighed naked
and alone in scales held by the Hand of God. Unjustified, it is drawn down by the
demons of its own unfulfillable desires, and thrust into torture-caverns beneath the
earth. Justified, a house containing book, scrolls and instruments of passion for the
rôle it may one day learn to play, is prepared for it by angels before the face of Christ.
The Old Serpent, representing the scale of matter in all its densities and time with its
corresponding speeds, stretches from hell, or the centre of the earth, into the presence
of Christ the sun.

At the bottom left, wise men are entering schools of regeneration upon earth, from
which some few fly directly—ignoring death and judgment—to the New Jerusalem,
or Inner Circle of Humanity, which stands on the level of God the Father. Above,
angels of time unroll the starry heaven of the Milky Way.

PLATE VI MEDIAEVAL JUDGMENT (CATHEDRAL OF BOURGES, 13TH CENTURY)
Under Christ the Judge, surrounded by the angels of sun, moon and planets,
the souls of the dead rise from their tombs to be weighed by the Archangel Michael.
As he weighs the grimacing evil personality of the dead man against his heart or
conscience, the angel protects with his other hand the child he must soon become.
To the left demons—whose faces in different parts of their bodies symbolize their
slavery to lower functions—carry off the damned souls to be melted down in hell.
To the right, the happy elect are led by angels through paradise into the bosom of
Abraham, that is, back into another time.

PLATE VII RENAISSANCE JUDGMENT (EL GRECO: BURIAL OF COUNT ORGAZ 1586)

Below, grave mourners point to the various parts of the dead man, while indicating with their other hands the destiny of each—head or personality vanishes, lower parts are consigned to earth, and heart to heaven. Along the border of the bishop's cope the shadows of himself in other lives pass through his brain. And the flame of solar energy, released by death, burns here and there among the onlookers, now as sex and now as consciousness. For these onlookers are none other than the man himself—in all his ages, all his 'I's.

Above, poised between earth and heaven, an angel already gathers from Christ, Mary and Joseph, the as yet shapeless embryo of another life; while Peter—his keys to the visible and invisible worlds making the symbol of infinity—and all the company of saints look on. And Peter, Joseph, saints and Christ are also he.

Reproduced by courtesy of Sir Robert Witt

(Opposite)

PLATE VIII SUFI TRANSFIGURATION (MIRĀJ FROM THE KHAMSA OF NIZAMI, BY SHAH MAHMUD NISHAPUR OF TABRIZ, 1539-43)

The Prophet, riding upon Buraq, the steed of conscious spirit, and led by the Archangel Gabriel, explodes from the molecular world of air into the electronic world of fire. Below him—inhabited by the souls of the Inner Circle—lie the fringes of the atmosphere, and far away the misty earth itself. Above, the light, fire, void and unity of the world of stars, from which gifts of knowledge, power and understanding come to him who, the face of individuality expunged, bursts beyond time into union with all creatures, all heaven and hell.

Reproduced by permission of the Trustees of the British Museum